e-Resource Management System for Libraries

The Author

Dr. Kailash D. Tandel, M.Com, M.L.I.Sc., M.Phil (Library Science), Ph.D (Library Science) SET is currently working as Assistant Librarian, (Assistant Professor equivalent), Vanbandhu College of Veterinary Science and Animal Husbandry and I/c University Librarian, Navsari Agricultural University, Navsari. He completed his B.L.I.Sc. with first rank from Veer Narmad South Gujarat University, Surat, Gujarat, He completed his M.L.I.Sc. with first rank from Saurashtra University, Rajkot, Gujarat and obtained his M.Phil (Library Science) with first rank and Ph.D (Library Science) from S.P. University, Vallabh Vidhyanagar, Gujarat. He has obtained M.Com. from Garda College, Navsari, Veer Narmad South Gujarat University, Surat, Gujarat.

Dr. Tandel has 15 years of experience in Library and Information Science and presented many papers in seminars/conferences. He has participated in several workshops and training programmes too. He has also organized State Level seminar and National Level workshop. His areas of interest are library Automation, Library Networking, Information System and Service, Library Management, Library Classification, Digital Library and Collection Building of e-Resources in Libraries.

e-Resource Management System for Libraries

– Author –

Kailash D. Tandel

2018

Daya Publishing House®

A Division of

Astral International Pvt. Ltd.

New Delhi – 110 002

Published by : **Daya Publishing House®**
A Division of
Astral International Pvt. Ltd.
– ISO 9001:2015 Certified Company –
4736/23, Ansari Road, Darya Ganj
New Delhi-110 002
Ph. 011-43549197, 23278134
E-mail: info@astralint.com
Website: www.astralint.com

Preface

Library services provide access to a huge range of electronic resources to support to studies, research and teaching. In this computer age, e-version of books, journals, etc or e-resources in general have become inevitable and hence it is very much needed to convert the printed version into e-version for future needs. Therefore, knowledge of the different e-resources, developing e-resources and preservation of them has become the need of this hour. Generally, e-resources may be classified into two major areas viz online e-resources and offline e-resources.

The development of e-resources requires the fundamental knowledge of the basic computer skills, Internet and Web skills and so on. E-Books are electronic forms of text that have been published in a digital format that displays on specialized reading devices or computers. Preservation of e-resources is as important as developing of them. This can be done with the help of online preservation i.e. virtual storage space in Gmail, Websites, Yahoo briefcase applications, Ringo. com applications for personal info, webshots.com for photos and so on and offline preservation i.e. floppy disks, compact disks, digital video disks, memory sticks, USB Flash Drive and Smart cards.

Thus the e-resources have significant roles to play in teaching and learning process and hence it is the high time for the teachers, librarians and students to get an awareness of these resources for their future academic growth.

An electronic resource is any information source that the library provides access to an electronic format. The present book is written to acquaint the readers to e-Resource Management System for Libraries. Greater emphasis is focused on access methods to electronic resources, challenges and opportunities of e-collection and management, use of e-resources: a boon to user of academic librarians, electronic books: an eco-friendly learning tools, electronic resources in higher education libraries and its familiarity and use of internet based e-resources and web services. It also covers laws of library science, trends, challenges and opportunities for LIS education, e-technology: a golden opportunities for farmers, fisheries and aquaculture, management of agricultural information and knowledge, application of social networking services for library, information security for academic library and protecting copyright in e-environment.

The information contained in this book would be an invaluable asset for the librarians, students and teachers in the field of library and information sciences, agriculture and fisheries. This book is also a valuable reference source for anyone interested in knowing more about electronic resource management system. I am grateful to all those persons as well as various books, manuals, periodicals, magazines, newsletters, journals, website etc. that helped in the preparation of this book.

In spite of the best efforts, it is possible that some errors may have occurred into the compilation and editing of the book. Further queries, suggestions and criticisms for improvement of the book are always welcome and shall be thankfully acknowledged. Last but not the least; it is a pleasure for us to extend our sincere thanks to Astral International Pvt. Ltd. for his keen interest shown in publishing of this book so efficiently and promptly.

Kailash D. Tandel

Contents

Chapter 1

An Introduction

e-Resources

An electronic resource is defined as a resource which require computer access or any electronic product that delivers a collection of data, be it text referring to full text bases, electronic journals, image collections, other multimedia products and numerical, graphical or time based, as a commercially available title that has been published with an aim to being marketed. These may be delivered on CD ROM, on tape, via internet and so on. Over the past few years, a numbers of techniques and related standards have been developed which allow documents to be created and distributed in electronic form. Hence to cope with the present situation, librarians are shifting towards new media, namely electronic resources for their collection developments that the documents of users are better fulfilled. The e-resources on magnetic and optical media have a vast impact on the collections of University libraries. These are more useful due to inherent capabilities for manipulation and searching, providing information access is cheaper to acquiring information resources, savings in storage and maintenance *etc.* and sometimes the electronic form is the only alternative.

E-resources (electronic resource) is that, "Information (usually a file) which can be stored in the form Electrical signal usually, but not necessary on a computer.

Types of e-resources: The e-resources are basically divided in two major types are:

1. Online e-resources, which may include:

☆ E-journal (Full text & bibliographic)

☆ E-books

☆ Online databases

☆ Web sites

2. Other electronic resources may include:

☆ CD ROM

☆ Diskettes

☆ Other portable computer databases.

Electronic: Defined by The Oxford Dictionary of New Words as an adjective relating to activities or processes mediated or enabled through the use of the computer, frequently by means of telecommunications links.

Internet: A network of networks which permit computers to communicate via a variety of languages called protocols. The internet may be used for electronic mail, discussion groups, file transfers, and web services. Protocols include FTP -file transfer protocol, HTTP - for the transfer of web pages from a server to a browser, and SMTP for e-mail transfer.

Web or World Wide Web (WWW): a portion of the Internet for the sharing of information using the HTTP protocol. It is incorrect to use it as synonymous with the Internet.

CD-ROM: Compact Disk-Read-Only Memory is a type of optical disk capable of storing large amounts of data which can not be erased. A single CD-ROM has the storage capacity of 700 floppy disks or 300,000 text pages.

Online Electronic Resources

"Librarians invest time and resources in creating reference Web sites, because doing so extends four familiar library service functions into cyberspace:

1. **Selection**
2. **Endorsement**
3. **Organization**
4. **Cooperation .". Steven W. Sowards (1998)**

A Typology for Ready Reference Web Sites in Libraries p.3 [http://www.firstmonday.org/issues/issue3_5/sowards/index.html]

The Library's acquisitions budget will be used to pay for license fees to access fee-based web sites Current research and instructional needs must be supported. Online resource selection shares many criteria outlined for both print and other types of electronic resources.

Online Resource Evaluation: Basic Criteria

☆ Does additional software have to be downloaded or purchased to make use of the resource?

☆ Is the web site well organized?

☆ Do the graphics and images support access to the substance of the resource?

☆ Do the table of contents or menus accurately reflect the content?

☆ Does the reputation of the source or sponsor of the site provide evidence for the accuracy of the information?

☆ If the site is a gateway, do the sites to which the links point have content relevant to the stated mission of the gateway?

☆ Is an e-mail address provided for the copyright/license holder, particularly in those instances when restrictions apply on the downloading of information?

☆ Is there clear evidence for the regular updating or maintenance of the web site?

☆ If a search engine is incorporated into the site, is it easy to use and does it support keyword (preferably Boolean) searching?

☆ Is the content scholarly, serious, and thorough?

☆ Is the site reliable, *i.e.* is it usually available, does the URL change infrequently, are the revisions and changes to the site genuine enhancements?

Web Sites - Open Access and Full-Text

This category of electronic resource constitutes the core of the LibGuides on the Articles& Research Databases page. Access is provided from the Library's homepage.

Selection

The web sites to which we establish links on our homepage are selected with the research needs of undergraduate and graduate students in mind and are intended to expand the range of resources available to these students. Particular attention will be paid to the following:

The information provided by the selected site will compensate for print monograph collections that are out of date and/or deficient in key subject areas. If significant to the subject of inquiry, attention will be paid to those scholarly, authoritative sites that have at least some Canadian content.

The selection will be of benefit to students who are studying from a distance or who are infrequent visitors to campus. Particular attention will be given to the needs of graduate level students who are enrolled in distance courses.

Organization

Once selected, each site will be carefully annotated by the Collections & Archives Librarian or the assigned Liaison Librarian with information of specific interest to our patrons.

Maintenance

Among the important factors to consider will be frequency of updates, change of content, redesign, reassignment of responsibility. At that time a decision will be made whether to retain or remove our link to the site, and if the link is retained, whether to revise the annotation in a LibGuide. Visitors to the Electronic Library will be encouraged to comment on the E-Library's content and organization, and suggest sites for possible inclusion.

Gateway

INFOMINE : Scholarly Internet Resource Collection

http://infomine.ucr.edu/

A cooperative effort of academic librarians to create a gateway to over 115,000 high quality scholarly education resources, both open access and fee-based, on the web. The advanced search and browse screen permits search strategies by field (keyword, description LCSH *etc.*), broad subject category, resource type.

Reviews

Internet Public Library

http://www.ipl.org/

Web site reviews with links can be located following a search path of increasing specificity *e.g.* subject collections>social sciences>education. IPL also provides access to sites maintained by associations. University of Michigan School of Information students work on its maintenance and enhancement.

The Scout Report

http://scout.wisc.edu/Reports/ScoutReport/

The Scout Report provides detailed information on its selection criteria based on evaluation of content, authority, maintenance, presentation, availability (*i.e.* do the links work ?) with a "very critical" look at for-fee sites. Subscribers to The Scout Report can contribute their own rating for each site. The Browse Resources page permits the identification of relevant sites pertaining to narrow subject areas.

BUBL

http://bubl.ac.uk/link

Based at Strathclyde University, this web site evaluation guide is aimed primarily at the academic community in the United Kingdom. Some international content is available. Advanced search supports Boolean. Each web site review is assigned a DDC number that can be used for searching purposes.

Web Sites - Bibliographic

In most instances the Library has chosen the electronic equivalent of indexing and abstracting services for which we had long established print subscriptions and that support the research and curricular needs of students and faculty at MSVU, *e.g.* Gender Studies Database and Hospitality & Tourism Index focus on the specialized programs offered at our institution.

Many of the reference databases to which we subscribe are aggregations, *i.e.* the vendor or aggregator conglomerates journals from several publishers under one interface and search engine. The inclusion of article full-text as part of the index is a significant feature of Academic Search Premier (Ebsco) and Academic Research Library (ProQuest). Among the features of aggregations to take into consideration are 1. the stability of content due to the requirement that the vendor negotiate rights from several publishers and 2. the embargoes on access to full-text articles in the most recent issues of some indexed titles.

Electronic Journals

Electronic or e-journals are defined in the Harrod's Librarians' Glossary as "journals in which all aspects of preparation, refereeing, assembly, and distribution are carried out electronically."

In most instances the electronic journals to which MSVU subscribes have been bundled with current print subscriptions. Recently we have elected to subscribe to some titles as e-journals only. Some major publishers that provide electronic journal access to faculty and students at MSVU are Wiley, Elsevier, Royal Society of Chemistry, Springer and the American Chemical Society.

Note: In most instances, print or print/electronic subscriptions will be retained if the only electronic source is an aggregator (*e.g.* ProQuest or Ebsco) - embargoes are unacceptable. The preferred source for an electronic journal is from the publisher of the title.

Once a subscription to an e-journal is initiated, the journal will be catalogued for Novanet.

The library budget will not be used to support access to e-journals from computer labs or faculty offices unless comparable access is available from public areas of the library.

Electronic Journal Evaluation: Basic Criteria

When selecting e-journals, the following should be considered:

☆ Does access require the purchase and loading of special software, or the purchase of additional hardware like printers?

☆ Are the pages marked up to support text images and links, or scanned to replicate the print version, or does more than one format co-exist?

☆ Can the user download the full-text to disk or print it? Can the entire article be downloaded / printed, or only a single screen at a time?

☆ Does the e-journal have an index? Does it support full-text searching?

☆ Does the e-journal have features which are not available in the equivalent print version *e.g.* interactive links or links from footnotes?

☆ Once access to the electronic version is provided will the equivalent print subscription be cancelled, and if so, will the access fee be affected?

☆ What is the e-journal's archival capacity? Who is responsible for maintaining the archives? What guarantees are in place for the retrieval of back files?

☆ Are there license agreements to be signed at the time of ordering? What mechanisms must be in place to prevent unauthorized use?

☆ How is the subscription rate determined: by the number of simultaneous users, the number of access points, the number of passwords or IP addresses, enrolment, the maintenance of an equivalent print subscription?

e-Journals: Collection Development Tools

Gateways

Serials in Cyberspace Collections, Resources, and Services.

http://www.uvm.edu/~bmaclenn/

A useful directory of web sites with information relating to e-journal acquisition and access arranged by country and institution.

Electronic Collection

http://www.collectionscanada.ca/electroniccollection/

Published Canadian books and journals that are accessible through the worldwide web. The collection may be searched by title, subject, or keyword. All publications are catalogued and archived by Library and Archives Canada

Data Files

For the purpose of the Collections Development Policy Manual, machine readable data files or MRDFs are defined somewhat narrowly as data files created at academic institutions for research purposes, or by government agencies for policy planning, and subsequently made available under license to researchers. The curricular and present or anticipated research needs of a sufficiently broad sector of the university community must justify the acquiring, archiving, and servicing of data files. At the very least, the license must give access to any member of the university community who can make use of the data for non-commercial purposes. Access to data files purchased or licensed for use by the Library should not be restricted to a single researcher.

Data Liberation Initiative (DLI)

http://www.statcan.ca/english/Dli/dli.htm

Provides university researchers and instructors not-for-profit use of a wide range of Statistics Canada data files and databases. The files may be distributed to member institutions on CD-ROM or downloaded via FTP from the DLI site by the University's designated DLI contact. Many data files are accessible from the server at the University of Western Ontario for DLI subscribers via Equinox.

A database of downloadable Statistics Canada Survey files (including the Censuses) has been made accessible to faculty and students at DLI member institutions. Researchers can access the Equinox site from work stations on campus, select variables of interest, download the data using a statistical package or, in many instances, display the data on screen in tabular form using Beyond 20/20 browser software.

Electronic Resource Funding

Most electronic resources, both multidisciplinary and subject-focused, are funded from the Library's acquisitions budget. This line provides funds for aggregated databases such as Ebsco's Academic Search Premier and Proquest Research Library and full-text databases such as the electronic journals collection published by Wiley InterScience.

Canadian Research Knowledge Network National Site Licence that provides access to scholarly databases (MathSciNet, Elsevier ScienceDirect *etc.*) is funded by its own line in the Library's acquisitions budget

Electronic Resource Licensing

A copy of the licensing agreement should be kept for easy referral in the appropriate department e..g. Reference or Serials, with a duplicate copy retained by the University Librarian. The head of each library unit is responsible for the submission of registration or warranty cards, and the maintenance of a file of documents pertaining to the resources purchased or licensed for use by the unit.

The University Librarian will review and sign licensing agreements, and will be consulted in decisions with respect to the lease or purchase of electronic data from acquisitions funds.

LIBLICENSE

http://www.library.yale.edu/~llicense/index.shtml

provides useful information and assistance for academic librarians as they read and negotiate licenses with information providers, with the caution that this is a U.S. resource with references to U.S. laws.

Electronic Resource Evaluation: General Guidelines

Electronic resources are selected using many of the same criteria adopted for the selection of monographs and serials. Please refer to "Monographs: Selection Criteria" and "Serials: Selection and Review" in the Collections Development Policy Manual. Obviously the fundamental question to address during evaluation is whether the resource will contribute to the strength of the collection and the quality of service to our patrons. Content and authority is usually weighed more heavily than design or operational features during the evaluation process.

Among general questions to consider with respect to both open-access and fee-based electronic resource selection:

☆ Is electronic or print the best medium to deliver the information?

☆ Will the electronic resource enhance instruction and/or the acquisition of knowledge?

☆ Does the product's interface and other features seem appropriate for, and usable by our patrons?

☆ Does the software allow for both printing and downloading?

☆ Will the resource require an excessive amount of time to learn and teach in order to be useful?

☆ Does it use a search engine similar to those already used by patrons?

☆ Do on-screen tutorials exist or will customized tutorials have to be prepared by reference / bibliographic instruction staff?

☆ Does the resource incorporate useful support materials ,*e.g.* thesauri of search terms, function-specific help screens?

☆ Are there similar resources available to compare with the one under consideration?

Hundreds with Brief Description

Authors browsed internet and other sources and selected these 100 e- prefixes with description which are as here under:

e-Attendance

E-Attendance is an electronic attendance system in which every employee makes their attendance in computer rather than using attendance book. The Electronic Time Attendance system tracks the entire employee related details including over-time, under-time, leave *etc.*

www.acct2k.com/eattendance.html

e-Agriculture

E-Agriculture (sometimes written eagriculture) is a relatively recent term in the field of agriculture and rural development practices. Food and Agriculture Organization (FAO) of the United Nations in 2006 identified "e agriculture" with information dissemination, access and exchange, communication and participation processes improvements around rural development.

www.e-agriculture.org

e-Bay

E-bay marketing (NASDAQ: EBAY) is an American internet consumer-to-consumer corporation that manages eBay.com, an online auction and shopping website in which people and businesses buy and sell a broad variety of goods and services worldwide.

www.ebay.in/

e- Billing

Electronic billing is the electronic delivery of invoices (bills) and related information by a company to its customers. Electronic billing is referred to by a variety of terms, a) Electronic bill payment. b) EBPP – Electronic bill presentment and payment. c) EIPP – electronic invoice presentment and payment.

www.ebs.in/

e- Book

An electronic book (variously, e-book, ebook, digital book) is a book-length publication in digital form, consisting of text, images, or both, and produced on, published through, and readable on computers or other electronic devices.

www.ebook.com/

e-Book Reader

An E-book reader, also called an e-book device or e-reader, is a mobile electronic device that is designed primarily for the purpose of reading digital e-books and periodicals.

www.en.wikipedia.org/wiki/E-book_reader

e-Business

Electronic business commonly referred to as "eBusiness" or "e-business", or an internet business, may be defined as the application of information and communication technologies (ICT) in support of all the activities of business.

www.en.wikipedia.org/wiki/Electronic_business

e-Banking

Online banking (or Internet banking) allows customers to conduct financial transactions on a secure website operated by their retail or virtual bank, credit union or building society. The precursor for the modern home online banking services were the distance banking services over electronic media from the early 1980s. These services started in New York in 1981.

www.en.wikipedia.org/wiki/Online_banking

e-Calibre

E-calibre is a free and open source e-book library management application developed by users of e-books for users of e-books. It has a cornucopia of features divided into the following main categories: library management, E-book conversion, syncing to e-book reader devices, downloading news from the web and converting it into e-book form, comprehensive e-book viewer, and content server for online access to your book collection.

www.calibre-ebook.com/

e-Card

E-card is similar to a postcard or greeting card, with the primary difference being that it is created using digital media instead of paper or other traditional materials. E-cards are made available by publishers usually on various Internet sites, where they can be sent to a recipient, usually via e-mail.

www.123greetings.com/

e-Child Care

E-Child Care is technology that will use either a telephone or a swipe card system to provide real time tracking and verification of child care attendance. It will automate and eliminate manual processes including paper invoices, and it will provide more efficient services to providers, including quicker payments. In addition, the system will provide a portal where providers can find out about a child's authorization, see that is registered at their center; obtain daily check in/out report and other reports on enrollment and attendance.

www.echildcare.com.au/

e-Choupal

E-Choupal is an initiative of ITC Limited, a large multi business conglomerate in India, to link directly with rural farmers via the Internet for procurement of agricultural and aquaculture products like soybeans, wheat, coffee, and prawns. This programme involves the installation of computers with internet access in rural areas of India to offer farmers up-to-date marketing and agricultural information.

www.echoupal.com/

e-Cigarette

An electronic cigarette (or e-cigarette, e-cig) is a cigarette substitute. It gives small amounts of the chemical nicotine without the tobacco or other chemicals from real cigarettes. The main substances making up in the liquid in the e-cigarettes are nicotine, propylene glycol, glycerin and some flavours or smells.

www.en.wikipedia.org/wiki/Electronic_cigarette

e-Cinema

The creation of movies in electronic formats rather than film, coined in the 1980s, the term referred to analog video at that time, both in standard format and high-definition such as the Japanese analog HD system. Later, electronic cinema evolved into digital cinema, and the two terms were used synonymously for a while.

www.ecinemasystems.com

e-Codices

E-codices are a Virtual Manuscript Library of Switzerland. The goal of the

e-codices project is to provide access to all medieval and selected early modern manuscripts of Switzerland via a virtual library.

www.e-codices.unifr.ch/

e-Collection

E-collection is the fourth Compilation album released by Brazilian rock band Titãs. It is a double album. The first CD features greatest hits of the group, and the second one, only rarities.

www.ecollection.ril.com/

e-Commerce

Electronic commerce, commonly known as e-commerce, ecommerce or e-comm, refers to the buying and selling of products or services over electronic systems such as the Internet and other computer networks. It also includes the entire online process of developing, marketing, selling, delivering, servicing and paying for products and services. The amount of trade conducted electronically has grown extraordinarily with widespread Internet usage.

www.en.wikipedia.org/wiki/Electronic_commerce

e-Corpus

E-corpus is a collective digital library that catalogs and disseminates numerous documents: manuscripts, archives, books, journals, prints, audio recordings, video, *etc.*

www.e-corpus.org/

e-Coupon

E-coupon, is the coupon in electronic form, refers the promotional voucher which according the various electronic media (including the Internet, MMS, SMS, *etc.*) to make, spread and use. It is mainly low-cost of production and dissemination and it is not only more convenient for users but also save marketing costs for businessmen, deeply welcomed by consumers and trade companies.

www.e-coupon.com/

e-Dictionary

An electronic dictionary is a dictionary whose data exists in digital form and can be accessed through a number of different media. Electronic dictionaries can be found in several forms.

www.edictionary.com/Cached - Similar

e-Directory

E-Directory is a hierarchical, object oriented database used to represent certain assets in an organization in a logical tree, including organizations, organizational units, people, positions, servers, volumes, workstations, applications, printers, services, and groups in electronic form.

www.edirectory.com

e-Discovery

Electronic discovery refers to discovery in civil litigation which deals with the exchange of information in electronic format (often referred to as electronically stored information or ESI).

www.en.wikipedia.org/wiki/Electronic_discovery

e-Education

Commonly referred to as online education, E-education is the process of learning online. A person looking to expand technical skills, Internet learning provides a boundary-free way to broaden the horizons. Many elite universities and technical schools offer online programmes.

www.en.wikipedia.org/wiki/E-learning

e-Emphasy

E-Emphasys Technologies is a global IT solutions company dedicated to helping equipment dealers and rental companies achieve profitable growth. Building on more than a decade of continuous growth and innovation, e-Emphasys technologies stands behind proven, comprehensive solutions that enable companies to increase revenue, reduce cost, and leverage innovation to gain competitive advantages.

www.e-emphasys.com/

e-Environment

In E-Environment the use and promotion of ICTs act as an instrument for environmental protection, sustainable use of natural resources, establishment of monitoring systems, to forecast and monitor the impact of natural and man-made disasters, particularly in developing countries, LDCs and small economies.

www.itu.int/ITU-D/cyb/app/docs/itu-icts-for-e-environment.pdf

e-Fax

The World's Online Fax Service. Fax by email using PC or Mobile. Archive faxes digitally. Fax from anywhere.

www.efax.com/

e-File

E-File is the term for electronic filing, or sending your income tax return from tax software via the Internet to the IRS or state tax authority. E-filed returns cost 20 times less to process compared to a paper return, which saves tax payers a lot of money.

https://incometaxindiaefiling.gov.in/

e-Freight

E-freight aims to take the paper out of the air cargo supply chain and replace it with cheaper, more accurate and more reliable electronic messaging. Facilitated by

IATA, the project is an industry-wide initiative involving carriers, freight forwarders, ground handlers, shippers and customs authorities.

www.iata.org

e-G8 Forum

E-G8 Forum (or simply the eG8) was an invitation-only summit of leaders in government and industry focusing on the Internet in the context of global public policy.

www.en.wikipedia.org/wiki/E-G8_ForumCached

e-Government

E-Government (short for electronic government, also known as e-gov, digital government, online government, or connected government) is digital interactions between a government and citizens (G2C), government and businesses/Commerce (G2B), government and employees (G2E), and also between government and governments/agencies (G2G).

www.en.wikipedia.org/wiki/E-Government

e-Gold

E-gold is a digital gold currency operated by Gold and Silver Reserve Inc. under e-gold Ltd., and allowed the instant transfer of gold ownership between users until 2009 when transfers were suspended due to legal issues. E-gold Ltd. is incorporated in Nevis, Saint Kitts and Nevis but the operations were conducted from Florida, USA.

www.e-gold.com/www.en.wikipedia.org/wiki/E-gold

e-Granth

Strengthening of Digital Library and Information Management under NARS (e-GRANTH)' is a subproject under component-1 of National Agricultural Innovation Project (NAIP), Indian Council of Agricultural Research (ICAR), New Delhi.

It provides digital access to library resources of 12 different research institutes and agricultural universities which include OPAC, important institutional repositories, rare books and old journals and makes them publically accessible over internet under NARS with Online Computer Library Center (OCLC) partnership.

www.egranth.ac.in/

e-Granthalaya

E-Granthalaya is library automation software of Department of Information Technology, Ministry of Communications and Information Technology, Government of India. Using this software the libraries can automate in-house activities as well as user services.

www.egranthalaya.nic.in/

e-Grantz

E-grantz is web based solutions for the timely disbursement of educational assistance to all the post matric students of SC, ST, OBC as well as economically weaker sections of society in Kerala. It provides provision for making online application, processing and sanction of educational assistance. This project benefited 3 lakhs students across 3463 educational institutions across the state and has brought transparency and accountability in the system.

https://www.e-grantz.kerala.gov.in/

Cachede-Gurukul

E-Gurukul is attempting to follow ancient tradition in current age. E-gurukul is endeavouring to bring the a) online courses in various categories – art, science, holistic living, courses for children and much more. b) live web sessions by various experts. c) live virtual web events and much more.

www.gurukul.edu/pdf/Issue29.pdf

e-GyanKosh

E-GyanKosh, IGNOU a National Digital Repository of India to store, index, preserve, distribute and share the digital learning resources developed by the open and distance learning institutions in the country.

www.egyankosh.ac.in/

e-Health

E-Health is a relatively recent term coined in 1999 for healthcare practice, healthcare practice using the Internet, health informatics and electronic/digital processes in health.

www.en.wikipedia.org/wiki/MHealthCached - Similar

e-How

E-how is an online how-to guide with more than 1 million articles and 170,000 videos offering step-by-step instructions. E-how articles and videos are created by freelancers and cover a wide variety of topics organized into a hierarchy of categories. Any E-how user can leave comments or responses, but only contracted writers can contribute changes to articles. The writers work on a freelance basis, being paid by article.

www.ehow.com/

e-Hundi

E-Hundi service allowed offering online donation. With e-Hundi service, anyone can offer online hundi donation on behalf of yourself and your near and dear ones in a very easy way.

www.ttdsevaonline.com/ehundi/ehundi.aspx

e-Informing

E-informing is gathering and distributing purchasing information both from and to internal and external parties using Internet technology.

www.diigubc.ca/research/egovernment/

e-Infrastructure

E-Infrastructure is the term used for the technology and organizations that support research undertaken in this way. It embraces networks; grids, data centres and collaborative environments, and can include supporting operations centres, service registries, single sign-on, certificate authorities, and training and help-desk services. Most importantly, it is the integration of these that defines e-infrastructure

www.jisc.ac.uk/media/documents/publications/einfrastructure_rtf.rtf

e-Ink

E Ink continues to revolutionize the E-paper market with E Ink Triton Imaging Film. These Color E-paper displays enabled by Triton deliver high-contrast, sunlight readable, low-power performance that further closes the digital divide between paper and electronic displays.

www.eink.com/display_products_triton.html

e-Journal

Electronic journals, also known as e-journals, e-journals, and electronic serials, are scholarly journals or intellectual magazines that can be accessed via electronic transmission. In practice, this means that they are usually published on the Web.

www.en.wikipedia.org/wiki/Electronic_journal

e-Laws

E-Laws provide access to official copies of Ontario's statutes and regulations. An official copy of a statute or regulation is an accurate statement of the law unless otherwise proved.

www.e-laws.gov.on.ca/navigation?file=home

e-Learning

E-learning comprises all forms of electronically supported learning and teaching. The term will still most likely be utilized to reference out-of-classroom and in-classroom educational experiences via technology, even as advances continue in regard to devices and curriculum. E-learning applications and processes include web-based learning, computer-based learning, virtual education opportunities and digital collaboration. Content is delivered via the Internet, intranet/extranet, audio or video tape, satellite TV, and CD-ROM.

www.en.wikipedia.org/wiki/E-learning

e-Lekha

E-Lekha is a prudent financial management application. It provides an electronic payment and accounting information system for the Civil Accounts Organization with the objective of improving efficiency and accuracy of the accounting process.

www.inclusion.in/index.php?option=com_content and view

e-Lessons

The e-lessons are designed to help teach dictionary skills to students. E-lessons containing dictionary activities for use in the classroom or for private study. Each

e-lesson comes complete with worksheet and teacher's notes. They have been specially written to work alongside a number of our dictionaries, including the Macmillan English Dictionary, the Macmillan Essential Dictionary and the Macmillan Collocations Dictionary.

www.esl.fis.edu/teachers/support/faq1.htm

e-Library

Electronic library is a web site which makes free copies of books available to visitors. Normally these books are classics which have no copyright restrictions. The term 'library' is not used in its strict sense, as once a book has been downloaded it is not returned.

www.elibrary.com/

e-LIS

E-LIS is an international Open Archive for Library and Information Science (LIS). Over 11,500 papers have been archived to date. It is freely accessible, aligned with the Open Access (OA) movement and is a voluntary enterprise. E-LIS has grown to include a team of volunteer editors from 44 countries and support for 22 languages.

www.eprints.rclis.org/

Cached - Similar e-Literacy

It offers individuals the potential to undertake commercial transactions and civic duties such as submission of tax returns, partake in the sharing of common interests that encompasses every pursuit from reading groups to e-dating. Clearly, e-literacy will soon become regarded as a key skill along with literacy and numeracy.

www.ics.heacademy.ac.uk/italics/vol5iss4/martin.pdf

e-Lock

E-Lock is a leading provider of digital and electronic signature solutions, empowering businesses across the globe to go paperless conveniently and securely. While ensuring security and legal compliance, our dSig and eSig solutions provide an easy, user-friendly way to authenticate documents, content and transactions.

E-Lock electronic and digital signature solutions can be integrated with any existing application, software or workflow.

www.elock.com/

e-Magazine

Electronic-magaZINE a magazine distributed to users via e-mail or the web. Pronounced "ee-zeen," it may be an electronic counterpart to a print subscription or be the only publishing method. No matter whether it is free or paid, e-zines require users to sign in as members. If text only, the e-zine is an e-newsletter, if published on a web site, it is a "webzine," while "zine" refers to all forms.

www.emagazine.com/

e-Mail

Electronic mail is an Internet service that allows those people who have an

e-mail address (accounts) to send and receive electronic letters. Those are much like postal letters, except that they are delivered much faster than snail mail when sending over long distances, and are usually free.

www.en.wikipedia.org/wiki/Email

e- Mall

In an e-mall, cyberspace is rented out cyber e-stores that wish to sell their goods. This store could be a specialized or generalized e-store.

www.e-mall.co.in/

e-Management

E"Management is a dedicated business division of HBM Group (est. 1991), with offices in reputable regulated Online Gaming Jurisdictions worldwide. They are a leading specialized turnkey provider of Business Support and Corporate Services to the Online Gaming Industry.

www.emanagement-group.com/

e-Marketing

E-Marketing or electronic marketing refers to the application of marketing principles and techniques via electronic media and more specifically the Internet. The terms E-marketing, Internet marketing and online marketing, are frequently interchanged, and can often be considered synonymous.

www.quirk.biz/

e-Marketsites

E-Marketsites expands on web-based ERP to open up value chains. Buying communities can access preferred suppliers' products and services, add to shopping carts, create requisition, and seek approval, receipt purchase orders and process electronic invoices with integration to suppliers' supply chains and buyers' financial systems.

www.bznas.com/showthread.php?t=158

e-Mitra

E-Mitra is an ambitious E-governance initiative of Government of Rajasthan, India which is being implemented in all 33 Districts of the state using Public-Private Partnership (PPP) model for the convenience and transparency to the citizen to deliver the services almost at their door- steps. www.emitra.gov.in/

e-Money

E-Money is also known as e-currency, electronic cash, electronic currency, digital money, digital cash, digital currency, cyber currency is money or scrip that is only exchanged electronically. Typically, this involves the use of computer networks, the internet and digital stored value systems. electronicHYPERLINK "http://en.wikipedia.org/wiki/Electronic_funds_transfer" funds transfer (EFT), direct deposit, digital gold currency and virtual currency, are all examples of electronic money.

www.en.wikipedia.org/wiki/Electronic_money

e-Music

E-Music is an online music and audio book store that operates by subscription. It is headquartered in New York City with an office in London and owned by Dimensional Associates. E-Music was one of the first sites to sell music in the MP3 format, beginning in 1998.

www.emusic.com/

e-Newsletter

An E-newsletter is a regularly distributed publication generally about one main topic that is of interest to its subscribers. Newspapers and leaflets are types of newsletters. Additionally, newsletters delivered electronically via email (e-Newsletters) have gained rapid acceptance for the same reasons email in general has gained popularity over printed correspondence. Many E-Newsletters are published by clubs, churches, societies, associations, and businesses, especially companies, to provide information of interest to their members, customers or employees.

www.enewslettersonline.com/

e-Notes

E-Notes offer a large resource of study guides, lesson plans, literary criticism, and a vibrant community of knowledgeable teachers and students in discussion forum.

www.enotes.com/

e-Paper

Electronic paper and electronic ink are a range of display technology which is designed to mimic the appearance of ordinary ink on paper. Unlike conventional backlit flat panel displays which emit light, electronic paper displays reflect light like ordinary paper.

www.en.wikipedia.org/wiki/Electronic_paper

e-Parliament

The E-Parliament is a non-profit organization that links together the world's democratic members of parliament and congress into a single forum. The intention is that this community of democratic legislators, together with interested organizations and citizens, can address a democracy gap at both the national and global levels.

www.e-parl.net/

e-Passport

Government of all countries has been quite focused on e-governance, on using the Internet to communicate, and other uses of technology. The e-passport was introduced and being doled out to the public. The conventional passport contains, name, address, age proof, but the new e-passport will have all the personal details, including finger-prints of the person carrying it.

www.watblog.com/2009/08/27/e-passports

e-Patients

E-Patients (also known as Internet Patient or Internet-savvy Patient) are health consumers who use the Internet to gather information about a medical condition of particular interest to them, and who use electronic communication tools (including Web 2.0 tools) in coping with medical conditions. The term encompasses both those who seek online guidance for their own ailments and the friends and family members (e-Caregivers) who go online on their behalf.

www.e-patients.net/

e-Payment

E-Payment facilitates payment of direct taxes online by taxpayers. To avail of this facility the taxpayer is required to have a net-banking account with any of the authorized banks.

https://onlineservices.tin.nsdl.com/etaxnew/tdsnontds.jsp

e-Portfolio

An electronic portfolio, also known as an e-portfolio or digital portfolio, is a collection of electronic evidence assembled and managed by a user, usually on the web. Such electronic evidence may include inputted text, electronic files, images, multimedia, blog entries, and hyperlinks.

www.eportfolio.org/

e-Procurement

E-Procurement (electronic procurement, sometimes also known as supplier exchange) is the business-to-business or business-to-consumer or business-to-government purchase and sale of supplies,work and services through the Internet as well as other information and networking systems, such as Electronic Data Interchange and Enterprise Resource HYPERLINK "http://en.wikipedia.org/wiki/Enterprise_Resource_Planning"Planning.

www.eprocurement.gov.in/

e-Profitbooster

E-Profitbooster is a place where a dedicated team is present to create comprehensive, internet-based, initiatives that extends value to customers, nurturing relationships and boosting profits. It is one of the fastest growing design solutions companies which provide Web designing, Web Branding Solutions, Web Applications and IT consulting projects.

www.e-profitbooster.com/

e-Rate

E-Rate is the commonly used name for the Schools and Libraries Programme of the Universal Service Fund, which is administered by the Universal Service Administrative Company (USAC) under the direction of the Federal Communications Commission (FCC). The programme provides discounts to assist most schools and libraries in the United States (and U.S. territories) to obtain affordable telecommunications and Internet access.

www.en.wikipedia.org/wiki/E-Rate

e-Reads

E-Reads are a trail-blazing re-printer of out-of-print genre and general fiction and nonfiction by leading authors. Books are available in all e-book formats and paperback. One can read the latest publishing news and provocative blogs by top commentators in the traditional and digital publishing fields.

www.ereads.com/

e-Republic

E-Republic, Inc. is leading publishing, research, event and new media company focused on the state and local government and education markets. E-Republic publishes the market's leading periodicals and websites, runs the largest intergovernmental conferences and produces over 100 targeted and custom events annually. A pioneer in intelligent media, E-Republic is an indispensable resource for public and private sector leaders building the public institutions that will shape the 21st century.

www.erepublic.com/

e-Research

E-Research (alternately spelled eResearch) refers to the use of information technology to support existing and new forms of research. It extends e-Science and cyber infrastructure to other disciplines, including the humanities and social sciences. It also includes research activities that use a spectrum of advanced Information and Communication Technology (ICT) capabilities.

www.e-research-global.com/

e-Retail

E-Retail Cybertech offers fully integrated retail automation solutions including store management systems and back office management systems for chain stores, franchise stores, supermarkets, hypermarkets and F and B outlets.

www.eretailtech.in/

e-Reverse auctioning

E-Reverse auctioning is using Internet technology to buy goods and services from a number of known or unknown suppliers.

www.en.wikipedia.org/wiki/Reverse_auction

e-School

E-School links enables schools to create a complete online learning community uniting teachers, parents, students and school professionals in the education process. It gives a school its own personalized website and allows principal and teachers through email links to communicate directly and securely with parents.

www.eschoolonline.com/Cached - Similar

e-Science

E-science is computationally intensive science that is carried out in highly distributed network environments, or science that uses immense data sets that require grid computing; the term sometimes includes technologies that enable distributed collaboration, such as the Access Grid. E-Science includes social simulations, particle physics, earth sciences and bio-informatics.

www.en.wikipedia.org/wiki/E-Science

e-Server

E-server provides managed hosting for the Microsoft platform. With expertise in technologies such as Citrix MetaFrame and Microsoft Terminal Services, E-server can also assist the business in extending applications beyond the desktop. E-server is dedicated to exceeding users expectations.

www.eserver.org/

e-Seva

Looking at 'service' from the citizens' point of view, the Government of Andhra

Pradesh, India seeks to redefine citizen services through e-seva, using state-of-the-art technologies. E-seva builds on the success of the TWINS pilot project launched in Banjara Hills, Hyderabad, in December 1999.

www.esevaonline.com/

e-Shopping

Online shopping is a form of electronic commerce whereby consumers directly buy goods or services from a seller over the Internet without an intermediary service. An online shop, e-shop, e-store, Internet shop, web shop, web store, online store, or virtual store evokes the physical analogy of buying products or services at a bricks-and-mortar retailer or shopping centre. The process is called business-to-consumer (B2C) online shopping.

www.en.wikipedia.org/wiki/Online_shopping

e-Signature

A signature is a stylized script associated with a person. An electronic signature, or e-signature, is any electronic means that indicates either that a person adopts the contents of an electronic message, or more broadly that the person who claims to have written a message is the one who wrote it (and that the message received is the one that was sent).

www.e-signature.com/

e-Society

E-Society is a society that consists of one or more e-Communities involved in areas from e-Government, e-Democracy and e-Business to e-Learning and e-Health, that use Information and Communication Technologies (ICT) in order to achieve a common interest and goals. It is a society that can be created by the extensive use of Information and Communication Technologies throughout the world.

www.en.wikipedia.org/wiki/E-society

e-Sourcing

E-Sourcing is a faster, more transparent and fairer way of facilitating tenders and conducting negotiations. Founded on a web-based platform, e-sourcing ensures smooth and clear communication, and is a more profitable business tool for the suppliers.

www.maersk.com/./e-Sourcing/Pages/What per cent 20is per cent 20e-Sourcing.as

e-Stamping

E-Stamping is a computer based application and a secured electronic way of stamping documents. It's an electronic way of paying stamp duty to the Government. The prevailing system of physical stamp paper/franking is being replaced by E-Stamping system.

www.stampduty.in/

e-Tax payment

E-Payment facilitates payment of direct taxes online by taxpayers. To avail of this facility the taxpayer is required to have a net-banking account with any of the authorized banks.

https://onlineservices.tin.nsdl.com/etaxnew/tdsnontds.jspCached

e-Tendering

E- Tendering is sending the requests for information and prices to suppliers and receiving the responses of suppliers using Internet technology.

www.e-tendering.com/

e-Texteditor

E is a new text editor for Windows, with powerful editing features and quite a few unique abilities. It makes manipulating text fast and easy and helps in focus on the writing by automating all the manual work.

www.e-texteditor.com/

e-Therapy

E-Therapy refers to the delivery of mental health services online. These online services are typically delivered in the form of email communications, discussion lists, live chat rooms, or live audio or audiovisual conferencing.

www.e-therapy.com.au/

e-Trading

Electronic trading company designed to provide investors with a service to actively manage their portfolios and execute trades at their discretion. Trades are executed with a computer or smart phone device and are made quickly. Typically a user will login to a website and make transactions. This data is then routed to appropriate dealers and exchange specialists.

www.en.wikipedia.org/wiki/Electronic_trading

e-Training

"E-Training" describes courses that anyone can take via the web, at any networked computer, at any time. Online training courses, such as those offered by different organizations allow learning at convenient times and places.

www.web.jjay.cuny.edu/etraining/whatis.html

e-Travel

Travel technology may also be referred to as E-Travel and electronic travel" or "electronic tourism". Travel technology is a term used to describe applications of Information Technology (IT), or Information and Communications Technology (ICT), in travel, tourism and hospitality industry.

www.etravel.co.in/

e-Tutor

E-Tutor is an accredited online school built on Dr. Martha Angulo's simple philosophy; students learn responsibility and are more engaged when given choices. It provides students a safe online learning environment to choose what and when they would like to learn next. While E-Tutor enforces basic rules to ensure that students are learning effectively, students are encouraged to set their own pace and to explore subjects that interest them.

www.e-tutor.com/

e-Twinning

The E-Twinning project aims to encourage European schools to collaborate using Information and Communication Technologies (ICT). The main concept behind E-Twinning is that schools are paired with another school elsewhere in the Europe. The two schools then communicate using the Internet (for example, by e-mail or video conferencing) to collaborate, share and learn from each other. www.etwinning.net/

e-Vedas

E-Vedas is an online library of vedic scriptures in the form of downloadable pdf files, which includes Bhagavad-Gita, Sri Isopanisad and many more.

www.e-vedas.com/

e-Verify

E-Verify is an Internet-based, free programme run by the United States government that compares information from an employee's employment eligibility verification form i-9 to data from U.S. government records. If the information matches, that employee is eligible to work in the United States.

www.en.wikipedia.org/wiki/E-Verify

e-Vite

E-vite is a social-planning website for creating, sending, and managing online invitations. E-vite was launched in 1998. The website is a free, advertisement-supported service. It was acquired by conglomerate IAC/InterActiveCorp in 2001. Liberty Media acquired it in 2010.

www.evite.com/

e-Voting

Electronic voting is a term encompassing several different types of voting, embracing both electronic means of casting a vote and electronic means of counting votes. It can involve transmission of ballots and votes via telephones, private computer networks, or the Internet.

www.en.wikipedia.org/wiki/Electronic_voting

e-Writing

E-Writing is the use of electronic circuits and electron devices to reproduce symbol such as an alphabet, in a prescribed order on an electronic display device for the purpose of transferring information from a source to a viewer of the display device.

www.e-writing.info/

Chapter 2

Access Methods to Electronic Resources

An Introduction

E-resources are part of the "Invisible Web" which is essentially information accessible through the Internet but normally can't be found on Google. Most e-resources are not freely available to everyone on the World Wide Web (exception are free or Open Access resources) and they may not appear on search engines like Google.

E-resource can be of following types:

☆ A bibliographic or full text database that allows you to search for relevant articles in your subject area

☆ A book, journal or newspaper that has been made available in electronic format

☆ A set of web pages

☆ A CD-ROM

Some other E- Resources are

☆ Off-computer access video,

☆ E-books,

☆ Electronic newspapers,

☆ Copyright issues for electronic information,

☆ Articles search,

☆ Electronic thesis,

☆ Mobile access to e-resources,

☆ Articles search video demonstration,

☆ Thesis collection and Audio-visual resources,

How to Access e-Resources

To access electronic journals, databases and e-books, you must be affiliated to the college or university library website or through internet IP address.

Access to e-Resources Within a Campus: It has to be preferably through IP authentication since password hinders the usage. For using outside of the campus, password can be used. There is good innovation in this connection that Athens provides a single user name and password to many online resources subscribed by the library. There are approximately 250 resources which are compatible with Athens (LEAHY). Athens is very popular in UK universities though its user population is spreading to other countries as well. Athens provides the user access to the resources anywhere in the world. While the campus users access through IP authentication system without any identification, for those who wish to use the e-resources outside the campus, Athens goes a long way towards removing the barrier to the use of various logins and passwords.

On-site Access

If you are at your institute library that has been managed with information technology infrastructure alongwith internet connection, most e-resources can be accessed directly (there is no requirement to enter a username and password). A few e-resources require an institutional login to access information. A small number of resources require a publisher supplied username and password. If so, a note in MetaLib states: "Publisher specific login details required". Check the password list for details.

Off-site Access

☆ E-resources can be accessed off-site by one of the following methods:

☆ Institutional or Library login– the new standard methodProxy server institutional login

☆ If you previously set the Athens cookie on your machine, you may find that you cannot login via UK Federation as you are forced to an Athens login. To remove the Athens cookie follow the instructions here.

Searching for e-Resources

☆ Metalib - a single point of access to all the Library's e-resources

☆ E-journals A-Z List - browse alphabetically or search by keyword

☆ Library catalogue - search both e-resources and print resources

☆ Articles search - a single, quick and easy search facility of the Library's online resources.

e-Journals

Use the A-Z link to discover our collection of 16,000 full text e-journals. You can search by journal title, subject, or look for a particular journal article. The A-Z link appears in the main menu at the top right of each screen Web. Access may be the result as:

☆ Individual electronic-only subscriptions.

☆ Multi-title electronic packages, bouquet of journals from publishers

☆ Electronic versions bundled with print subscriptions (*i.e.* where electronic full text available only to print subscribers) example science direct.

☆ Aggregate products from information providers such as Ebsco, Gale, and ProQuest (the library has no control over the content of these collections)

☆ Free access (these are not always catalogued, and may be linked only from a subject web page).

☆ Library maximises access to e-journals by several means:

☆ Cataloguing; bibliographic and holdings records and associated hypertext links through websites.Catalogued e-journals are also listed alphabetically by title on Library website.

☆ Organizing awareness programmes like Circulars, Pamphlets, Brochures, *etc.*

☆ Support and training to optimise use.

The selection of the e-journals basically depends on the needs of the institutes by the Vice-Chancellor/Directors/Dean with recommendation of Selection committee constituted with teachers/scientist and librarians. The library staff and students/ users also may offer suggestions to the appropriate collection. Librarian will consider the following criteria when selecting a new electronic-title or transferring a subscription from print to electronic or from one electronic version to another:

☆ Coverage and the timely availability of material.

☆ Enhanced contents and additional functionality of electronic as compared to print version.

☆ Convenience for users, *e.g.* unrestricted access in terms of location and time.

☆ Reliability of access

☆ Full-text availability in PDF and/or HTML or SGML

☆ Cost–effectiveness, like subscription savings, lower handling and overhead costs, numbers of simultaneous users included in licence terms.Guaranteed access to a complete file of titles for the years of the subscription.

☆ Publisher commitment to maintaining web access to a permanent archive of back-issues.

☆ Availability of usage statistics to enable rational decisions on future title additions or deletions.

Electronic Books

The books are available on the net or as fixed subscription licence code no. The selection, acquisition and delivery of electronic books can be accessed on following basis:

☆ Individual or collections of electronic-only books, ordered directly from the publisher or through a vendor.

☆ Electronic versions available with print purchases.

☆ Electronic books available freely on the web (not always catalogued)

Library Access of Electronic Books

The library maximises access of electronic books by several means:-

☆ Cataloguing: normal bibliographic records will be created for electronic books. Users will be able to access the full text via a link created through WEB OPAC.

☆ Loading and maintaining necessary software with the library.

☆ Providing access to software, for the clients of university/institute to download and install.

☆ Organizing awareness programmes like circulars, pamphlets, brochures, *etc.*

☆ Support and training to optimise use.

Selection of e-Books

The selection of the E-books decisions rest with Vice-Chancellor/Director with recommendation of Selection Committee constitute with teachers, scientists, students and librarian. The library staff and users may offer suggestions for appropriate collection. Questions relating to price and availability should be directed to the acquisitions department. Collection managers will consider the following criteria when selecting an electronic title, whether new or the equivalent of an existing print title in the collection:

☆ Demand of the users

☆ Suitability to curricular support

☆ Currency and comprehensiveness

☆ Cost, *e.g.* lower handling and overhead costs, number of simultaneous users included n licence terms.

☆ Enhanced contents and additional functionality.

☆ Ease of use and convenience for users, *e.g.* unrestricted access in terms of location and time.

☆ Reliable, stable and permanent access

☆ Appropriateness of formate, *e.g.* file size, supprted software clients.

☆ Availability of usage statistics to enable rational decisions on future title additions or deletions.

Electronic resources include CD-ROM/DVDs, bibliographical, abstracting, indexing databases, statistical, geographical information databases, multimedia databases include images, movies, documentary films, audio and video databases, directories, dictionaries, encyclopedias, animations, *etc.* Some other Electronic resources may include Government documents, working papers, conference proceedings, websites, image files, *etc.* These can be accessed through library website by authorised users out of library premises.

Subject Specific Databases

One of the best ways to find current and detailed information for projects and research is by using a subject-specific database. These contain citations and links to a variety of materials, including journal articles, conference proceedings, reports, web-based material and book chapters. You can access and search individual subject databases, or create custom sets of databases to search simultaneously, from the Find Databases link at the top right of each screen.

Advanced Article Search

To help find what you're looking for faster, try the Advanced Search option. This provides a more targeted search using specific fields (title, author, publisher, subject etc). You can also limit your search by publication date, resource type, and language. Sign in with your Service account. The fullest possible range of resources provided by the library.

Various Traditional Methods

☆ Access e-books through library OPAC (Online Public Access Catalogue). Some library automation packages do allow the integration of e-books metadata with library OPAC-provided metadata in the standard format. Integration allows a single point of search both for print and e-books.

☆ A to Z list of Journals: providing a list of e-journals subscribed and providing a direct link to the journals either from the library homepage or from the OPAC. This will ensure that the user does not miss out a particular periodical though it is hidden in a database. Such periodical list can be made alphabetically title-wise.

☆ Subject guides compiled by the library staff comprising of evaluated printed and e-resources. These subject guides are put on the library website. *e.g.* University of Dellaware Library Subject guides

☆ http://www.2lib.udel.edu/subj/(Accessed on 24.1.2009)

☆ http://www.lib.polyu.edu.hk/(Accessed on 25.1.2009)

☆ Some libraries bring out course-specific subject guides as banners, poster, brochures, bookmarks, e-mails, *etc.* Use of printed brochures, flyers, posters, book marks, *etc.* should not be underestimated. Such flyers, brochures, book marks, *etc.* be made freely available in various service points in the library. Posters be pinned in library, hostels, faculties meeting places *etc.* Various e-journal publishers have brought out templates of banners, posters, brochures, book marks, e-mails and press releases which can be used for publicizing their e-books.

When researchers have made recommendations about other interesting references, this tab will appear in each of your search results. Select the Suggestions tab to display a list of these references and full-text access options. Electronic publishing is a boon for modern readers of present era. It has certain advantages and disadvantages. If each of these advantages is overcome with advantages and the product will be 'user-centred' rather the, 'library centred' or 'publisher centred'. The challenge of this new direction in collection development policy is indeed an opportunity to serve better to the library.

Chapter 3

Laws of Library Science

Introduction: An Overview

The laws of library science were enunciated by Father of Library Science in India Dr. S.R. Ranganathan. These are fundamental laws numbering five. These laws have a sway over the entire discipline, *i.e.*, library science. They help in resolving any conflict that may arise during the functioning of libraries. These laws are guide for the library staff in deciding what is right and what is wrong in given situation or coming situation for taking decision.

These laws of library science came in force in the year 1928 and a detailed account of these laws and their implications was given in the form of a book by Ranganathan in 1931. These laws are:

1. First Law   :   Books are for use;
2. Second Law   :   Every reader his/her books;
3. Third Law   :   Every book its reader;
4. Fourth Law   :   Save the time of reader/staff;
5. Fifth Law   :   Library is a growing organism.

1. First Law: Books are for Use

The first law constitutes the basis for the library services. Ranganathan observed that books were often chained to prevent their removal and that the emphasis was on storage and preservation rather than use. He did not reject the notion that preservation and storage were important, but he asserted that the purpose of such activities was to promote the use of them. Without the use of materials, there is little value in the item. By emphasizing use, Ranganathan refocused the attention of the field to access-related issues, such as the library's location, loan policies, hours and days of operation, as well as such mundanities as library furniture and the quality of staffing. Previously the libraries were located at uneasy reach places of the locality of the city or town so that the library be kept free from dust and away from all sorts of people. It was looked like a show piece of the society. But according to, first law of library science, the library must be at the centre place of the city or academic institutes. In some colleges and universities, library was located in the room which is regarded as unfit for anything else so as to put them to use. Now-a-days main structure front areas are occupied for library. Previously it was the general concept that libraries were opened only on selected days in a week or month. But now it is opened on every office day and even on Sunday and holidays. And also after office hour it has been managed to open for needful people or students in the educational institutions. The library furniture and all things of arrangement of books should be modern as per the first law of library science as the environment affects the mind of the readers so the furniture of the libraries must be attractive and comfortable. There must be separate reading room and hospitality system like toilets, retiring rooms, canteen facility in the library premises.

As per the first law of library science, in the library there sufficient qualified library staff. Only librarian cannot do all the day to day work of library. Hence sufficient number of staff must be there as per the services of the library. The status of the librarian should be like a manager of the library and as a teacher in the academic institutes like college and universities. There is the total responsibility of the library staff to provide required documents to the needful reader like right book to right reader at right time. Readers not only come for books but they should be well acquainted with the librarian and other library staff to get proper guidance and direction regarding how to use the library.

2. Second Law of Library Science: Every Reader his/her Book

This law suggests that every member of the community should be able to obtain the library books and other needful materials available in the library. Ranganathan felt that all individuals from all social environments were entitled to library service, and that the basis of library use was education, to which all were entitled. These entitlements were not without some important obligations for both libraries/ librarians and library patrons.

Librarians should have excellent first-hand knowledge of the people to be served. Collections should meet the special interests of the community, and libraries should promote and advertise their services extensively to attract a wide range of readers. In the good olden days, education and privilege of learning rarely crossed occupational and income lines. Some said, "too much knowledge is dangerous and libraries may become the political centre. When a library school was started in Moscow, they asked as to "how the government tolerates library curses which pave the way for revolution." The men and the women have equal right to the library. It is not merely the income line that has divided the humanity, sex is another example that restricted the enforcement of the second law. In India also there is still this barrier. Girl child is deprived in comparison to the chilled. St. Paul said, "Women are inferior dependent class." Chesterfield was of the opinion that "Women are children of a larger growth." Experiments now reveal that women are as competent intellectually as the men to undertake any and all human vocations. All books have a perfect right of going to the hands of women. City folk and country folk: right of country folk to book came to be respected in most of the countries these days. It is said that "India live in villages" and rural libraries have to play an important role in bringing changes in agricultural practice industries, rural hygiene, health and family welfare. Village library has to be the nerve centre of social activities like musical concerts, lectures, dramas, exhibitions, audio-visual shows, *etc.*

The village librarian has to play an important role in dissemination of information to the villagers. He should use local fairs and festivals in popularising the library as a source of knowledge. Special libraries are to be established to cater to the information needs of patients in hospitals, prisoners, blind and other physically handicapped.

3. Third Law of Library Science: Every Book its Reader

This principle is closely related to the second law but it focuses on the item itself, suggesting that each item in a library has an individual or individuals who would find that item useful. Ranganathan argued that the library could devise many methods to ensure that each item finds it appropriate reader. One method involved the basic rules for access to the collection, most notably the need for open shelving. There required readers for every books whatever are available in the library. This law urges that an appropriate reader should be found for every book. Open access system in the library influence the readers to select the books freely as per their interest. The readers should have free access to the books in the library. He should feel free to move in the stack-room and lay hand on any book at his will and pleasure. Open access provides opportunities to readers to discover books which he never expected to have. Less used books are that way put to use. Library staff should display all new books in a proper manner, so that reader could discover and use them.

Most readers have no definite approach, which will take a shape only on seeing and handling a book. Shelf arrangement plays an equally important role in an open access library in canvassing for books. Subject arrangement on selves; a special shelf for displaying recent arrivals; and novelty in arrangement and display will attract the attention of the users. Library catalogue provides useful information about books and help in their selection. Now the online catalogues are also available in the computerised libraries. The cross references help the readers in location and selection of the required books.

Reference Work: with the classified arrangement, shelf arrangement and catalogue entries, there is the need for 'human factor'. The reference librarian should act as a canvassing agent for books. Books are mute and inert. They cannot select a match. It is the duty of a reference librarian to act like a marriage match-maker. He should find suitable readers for each and every book. It is the duty of reference librarian that he should always be in touch with readers to attach them with the available books in library stock. The reference librarian should publicize the value of books; role of the library as a social institution; library services, *etc.* He should make use of mass media like press, radio, television, public lectures, demonstration tours, exhibitions, library weeks, brochures and leaflets, special library publications, *etc.* for publicizing the library. The reference librarian should play an important role in book-selection. Proper and timely, local demands, local history, local needs as well as individual needs are to be considered while selecting books.

4. Fourth Law of Library Science: Save the Time of the Reader

Saving the time of staff is regarded as a corollary to this law. This law recognizes that the excellence of library service is its ability to meet the needs of the library users efficiently. To this end, Ranganathan recommended the use of appropriate business methods to improve library management. He observed that centralizing the library collection at one location provides distinct advantages. He also noted that excellent staff would not only include those who possess strong reference skills, but also strong technical skills in Cataloguing, cross-referencing, ordering, accessioning, and the circulation of materials.

Open Access Vs. Closed Access

In a closed access system, there will be a good loss of time in going through the catalogue. It is a greater difficulty, in the cause of a shelf or book catalogue. In big libraries, waiting at the counter to get a book may take a longer time, sometimes stretching into a few hours. This may be on account of many causes – the slip may be returned with the comment 'entry incorrect', 'On – loan', 'engaged', *etc.* Open access saves all these problems. It also saves the time of the staff.

Shelf-Arrangement

The more useful methods of shelf arrangement save much time of the reader. Arrangement by subject has been found to be useful and easy to locate a book. The subject represented in an artificial language of ordinal numbers is proved to save the time in locating the books. It has been the practice in libraries to arrange books in great demand at the entrance. This type of broken order is found to save the time of the users. Subjects with less number of books be given broad classification. This will help in locating books on the same subject at one place in the catalogue.

Stock Room Guide

Proper guide in the stack room will save the time of the users. At the entrance there should be a large, broad plan of the library to help the readers in locating the section in which they are interested. There should be a 'signal guide' on each rack. Inclusive class numbers be provided on the shelf plank. The tags on the books should best in a line (1″ above the bottom) so that it will be convenient for the eye.

Catalogue/Bibliography

Catalogue should have necessary and sufficient number of analytical entries and cross-references. Complete set of added entries be provided. Cooperative and centralised Cataloguing also saves the time of the readers. Topical bibliographies, cumulative indexes to journals, national and regional bibliographies, union catalogues, computerised databases, national networks, *etc.*

Reference Services

Assistance to users by way of invitation of freshman; guidance to the users; ready and long range reference assistance; help in selection of books; documentation services like indexing, abstracting, translating, reprography; information services like current awareness services, selective dissemination of information, referral services, information consolidation and repackaging, *etc.* will definitely help in the dissipation of research potential of the nation.

Circulation System

Two cards system is found to save the time of the readers over 'Daybook and Ledger' system. Computerised circulation system will further save the time of the users.

5. Fifth Law of Library Science: Library is a Growing Organism

This law emphasises more on the need for internal change than on changes in the environment itself. Dr. Ranganathan argued that library organizations must accommodate growth in staff, the physical collection, and patron use. This involved allowing for growth in the physical building, reading areas, shelving, and in space for the catalogue. The fifth law enunciates a fundamental principle that should govern the planning and organisation of libraries. It is an accepted fact that growing organism alone will survive.

Chapter 4

Trends, Challenges and Opportunities for LIS Education

Introduction: An Overview

Education is one of the largest activities in the world. It is as important as any other resource for the nation's economic and industrial development because it is the key to human resource development. Knowledge explosion and information explosion have expanded the catchment areas of learning at such a rapid pace that any field becomes obsolete in less than a decade. Library supplements a great deal in achieving educational goal and serves as a gateway for academic world. Libraries in general play an important role in the socio- economic and educational development of the state. Library is a social institution, the development of the libraries led to the development of a state as well as the nation. The library and information science profession requires a systematic education to make them dedicated for the cause to serve the humanity for the all round development. Depending upon the prevailing educational system, the library science education has undergone changes since its beginning in the nineteenth century. Graduate, undergraduate and PG programmes in library and information science are growing in size and scope. The present programmes like CLS/DLIS/BLIS/MLISc/M.Phil/Ph.D are recognized by UGC. Many colleges and universities recognize the importance of this dynamic field and have invested significant new resources into these programs. Their shapes increasingly reflect the academic culture in which they exist. Library and information science has now become a recognized discipline of study like any other.

Library Science refers to "The professional knowledge and skill with which recorded information is selected, acquired, organized, stored, maintained, retrieved, and disseminated to meet the needs of a specific clientele, usually taught at a professional library school." Information Science deals with "The systematic study and analysis of the sources, development, collection, organization, dissemination, evaluation, use, and management of information in all its forms, including the channels (formal and informal) and technology used in its communication."

Library and information science is the combination of library science and information science. Very often, library science is considered as traditional area of study and information science is regarded as advanced field of study that deals with different aspects of information, involving application of ICT in a great deal. Library and Information Science (LIS) provides education for library and information professionals. It aims at creating appropriate human resources to run the libraries and information centres such as Librarians, Information officer and Documentation Officer. It is just a question of preference. In actual practice, there are no hard and fast rules. LIS education is a life-long process. After initial formal education, it continues in the form of continuing education and staff development.

Sceinario of Library and Information Science Education

India would be one among the first five countries, imparting Library and information science (LIS) education in the world. Currently, LIS education is being imparted by a variety of institution which include universities, (traditional/ deemed), affiliated colleges, polytechnics, professional association, documentation centres, *etc.* Presently, there are about 120 universities, in India offering LIS education at various levels, and 63 universities offering doctoral degree in LIS (Ramesha and Ramesh Babu, 2007). The LIS education in India is offered at various levels such as certificate, diploma, degree, Associateship in Information Science (AIS), M.Phil. and Ph.D. These programmes are offered on regular basis as well as through correspondence courses or distance education.

Objective LIS Education

☆ To have a broad perspective on the principles of librarianship and information provision;

☆ To comprehend the principle underlying the organization, retrieval and management of information;

☆ To have an understanding of the management of libraries and other information agencies;

☆ To make them aware of the importance of information flow to the society.

☆ To have enhanced practical skills in ICT;

☆ To pursue in a variety of library and information service contextsTo provide them information about theories of library administration and organisation.

☆ To master the WWW;

☆ To leave with marketable links; To face the crucial challenges of ICT;

☆ To persue in a variety of liberary and information service contexts

☆ To meet the existing demands of the new information era;

Need of LIS Education in India

✩ Behavioural attitudes and understanding and information needs of individuals and institutions; Extensive theoretical and practical knowledge of information management and business;

✩ Extensive theortical and practical knowledge of information management and business;

✩ Problem solving methodology;

✩ Financial and quantitative methods of analyzing organizational information;

✩ Analytical abilities and critical thinking expertise;

✩ Information management in various professional contexts.

✩ Practical experience in information retrieval, indexing, cataloguing and classification of information resources;

✩ Analytical abilities to access information and to understand the principles of the organization of knowledge;

✩ In depth understanding of information organization, marketing and using information retrieval systems;

✩ Research theories and practices

✩ Competence in information handling

✩ Online information skills and Expertise in the use of electronic information;

Human Resource Management and Quantitative Practices and Management

(1) **Job Market:** The job market for library professional appears to be high in India Graduates with ICT skills seem to have better job opportunities in the private sector than in libraries.

(2) **Growing Demand in Other Information-Related Fields:** While it is true that the demand for librarians is not as strong as other fields, there are many other positions for which you can be very well suited with this degree. Someone with strong research and analytical skills can find strong employment possibilities in other fields, including market research and computer system management.

The Bureau of Labour Statistics shows that the demand for computer and information systems managers is going to grow by 18 per cent by 2020, which is faster than average when compared to other positions. Growth in this field is being fuelled by organizations that are improving their information technology, and they need strong managers of data and information to lead these projects.

(3) Information management recognized as an important discipline.

(4) **Trends Among Educators:** The number of faculty members with a doctoral degree is increasing in India. Many of them obtained doctoral degrees

from different universities in India and abroad. As a result, more faculty members want to teach newly developed areas in informatics such as knowledge management as well as the theoretical aspects of classification, ontology, and taxonomy, rather than traditional topics in librarianship. This has strengthened LIS education and led to some LIS programs inviting professional Librarians to teach traditional topics as adjunct faculty.

(5) **LIS Curriculum:** Some of the LIS schools in India have strong curriculum for Master Degree in LIS which includes information technology concepts such as imaging technologies; Optical character recognition; Mark-up languages, including HTML, SGML, XML; Cataloguing and metadata; Indexing and DB technology; Web technology.

Weaknesses of LIS Education

(1) **Non-existent of accreditation bodies:**In order to achieve academic excellence it is essential to have standards and norms of LIS education. Innumerable LIS schools are being established without following minimum standards and norms.

(2) **Emerging of new LIS Schools:** There is an ever increasing growth of new LIS schools all over India. These are either formal, non-formal, or in distance mode. Many of these schools do not have minimum basic facilities. Emergence of such types of institutions has led to the production of sub-standard library professionals. It leads to the creation of more and more problem of unemployment in the job market.

(3) **Insufficient Faculty Strength:** Even in the present century there are some library schools in India which have still majority of faculty manned by part-time teachers with the University Librarian as the head. University Grants Commission (UGC) Review Committee, 1965, had the practice of employing library staff of the university as part-time teachers and recommended one reader and two Lecturer for a department conducting BLISc course, and one Professor, two Readers and four Lecturers for a department conducting MLISc course.

(4) **Dual responsibility:** Λ few Professors of LIS Departments in India are also in-charge of the University Library. This is not a healthy practice. The present day librarians, on the other hand, are having tremendous responsibility and involvement in their day to day work.

(5) **Medium of Instruction and Employability of LIS students:** There are serious considerations associated with this choice of medium. Today's Indian LIS job world has become more sophisticated where communication skills matter much and it also helps the candidates to seek job anywhere in India and also abroad.

(6) **Inadequate library facilities:** The Library, for library science students is like a workshop or a laboratory to do practical assignments, learn and create new things. In India some LIS schools have either no library at all,

or a library with adequate collection of text-books, reference books and practical tools (classification schemes, cataloguing codes and list of subject headings).

(7) **Lack of IT Laboratory facilities:** UGC Model curriculum committee (2001) has strongly recommended that apart from enriching the contents, it is necessary that LIS departments have an IT laboratory with network facilities. Competent professionals cannot be produced with merely theoretical exposition; they require adequate practical exposure by working in a well-developed computer laboratory. Practical training for computerized routines such as provision of information services, internet access, Online and CD ROM searching, *etc.*, is required.

(8) **Curriculum updating:** Many LIS schools in India hardly revise and update their syllabus in a regular basis. These syllabuses are needed to be restructured to accommodate emerging changes in the field of knowledge. If well designed curricula are adopted and implemented, we may expect quality education suitable both for the practicing library professionals.

Major Opportunities for LIS Education

(1) Opportunity to Enhance Information Professionals' Social Standing: Librarians in several countries face low social recognition and poor conditions, particularly in public libraries. This trend may have been caused by the poor professional orientation in our society and culture as well as a lack of professionalism on the part of librarians. This will lead students to seek information related jobs in business rather than in professional librarianship. Therefore, in this knowledge society LIS education in India need to establish a strong professional basis for information professionals, including librarians, so as to make our libraries more supportive of our information/knowledge oriented society.

(2) IT Oriented LIS Course: IT era brought tremendous changes in every field. Library science is no exception to it. In an information- and knowledge-oriented society, librarians and information Professionals need to develop the required knowledge and skills to take advantage of ICT. These needs have driven the shift of LIS education from traditional librarianship toward ICT-oriented informatics. It is good opportunities for LIS schools to go for an IT oriented LIS course and have changed the names of their LIS programs from library science to information science.

(3) Librarians Role in Today's World: 1. Librarian/Deputy Librarian/ Assistant Librarian/Library Assistant 2. Reference Librarian 3. Archives and Manuscripts Librarian 4. Bibliographer 5. Business Information Coordinator/Specialist 6. Cataloguer/Metadata executive 7. Content Manager/Editor/Web Site Coordinator/8. Information Advisor/Analyst/ Associate/Broker/Manager/Information Officer/Research Analyst/ Specialist/Information Research Specialist 9. Digital Facilitator/Librarian 10. Document Officer/Document Analyst/Specialist 11. E-Learning co-coordinator/Specialist 12. Knowledge manager/Specialist/Analyst *etc.*

Threats to LIS Education

☆ Good students are not admitting to LIS course because lack of publicity and impact of engineering, medical and technological education *etc.*

☆ Attracting students to traditional LIS programs has been very difficult, and curricula and education systems take into account the needs of the information industry as a whole. Therefore, the present LIS curricula should include IT applications which may make the course more IT oriented. IT application in LIS education is a major threat.

☆ All the LIS schools in India should develop excellent curricula to meet the knowledge challenges of the 21st century otherwise there is chance of split LIS graduates into traditional and IT intensive role which is another threat to LIS education. Therefore, Revamping of curriculum redesign curriculum to accommodate changes and new trends.

Emerging Trends of LIS Education

☆ Departments have started establishing their own computer labs and are emphasizing upon practical training on the use of IT, making the students competent to work effectively and efficiently in the electronic information environment.

☆ Departments are carefully viewing their curriculum to put more emphasis on emerging areas like computer and communication technologies, and reducing emphasis on traditional techniques like Classification and Cataloguing.

☆ The beginning of PG Diploma course in some specialized areas, like Archival and Documentation Management, Library Automation, Networking and Information Technology *etc.*,

☆ The trend offering two year integrated course in emerging to eliminate duplication of course contents at BLIS and MLIS level and providing sufficient time for teaching computer and communication technologies relating it to library work through practical training.

☆ More LIS departments are getting independent status and privileges like other departments of the university in terms of full-time teachers and full-time head.

☆ To face the technological challenges, more existing faculty members are engaging themselves in computer and IT related courses. New faculty positions are created and filled up with the LIS professionals having computer and IT related qualifications.

☆ A growing number of LIS departments are developing their own websites to provide information about them. With the growing impact of the internet on LIS, new areas such digital libraries, electronic publishing, online resources, metadata and information architecture are reckoning as nascent field of LIS research.

Course Objectives

Certificate/Diploma

Objectives

1. To expose students about the concept of library, its types, objectives and functions
2. To acquaint elementary technical operations associated with a small library
3. To motivate/encourage towards a career in librarianship.

BLISc

Objectives

1. To familiarize students the concept of librarianship and information science.
2. To appraise different management tools and techniques to be applied in libraries and information centres.
3. To expose students different components of information technology and its application in LICs.
4. To make aware of various sources of information.

MLISc

Objectives

1. To acquaint and expose the students about the trends and developments in information society.
2. To familiarize different modes and patterns of information seeking behavior of the users to developed expertise in the analysis, organization and consolidation of information.
3. To provide advance ICT knowledge and its application in LICs.
4. To understand the importance of quantitative techniques including statistical methods.

M.Phil.

Objectives

1. To make an advancement of knowledge and contribution to new ideas in the library and information science.
2. To apply different methods of research design to find solutions to the problems, formulate research proposals.
3. To demonstrate an innovative and scientific research in library and information science.

Ph.D.

Objectives

1. The objective of the Ph.D programme is to allow a researcher to work independently in a specialized area of knowledge.
2. To make contributions to innovative an original ideas to suggest modifications in the existing practices in the areas of library and information science

List of Universities (Regular Mode)

LIS Education is conducted by many Institution/Schools/Universities in India. List of universities offering LIS education through Conventional mode:

☆ University of Delhi, Delhi.

☆ Jamia Millia Islamia Jamia Nagar New Delhi.

☆ Kurukshtra University, Haryana.

☆ University of Jammu Jammu.

☆ University of Kashmir Hazrathal, Srinagar.

☆ Guru Nanak Dev University, Amritsar.

☆ Panjab University, Chandigarh.

☆ Panjabi University, Patiala.

☆ Aligarh Muslim Universtiy, Aligarh.

☆ Babasaheb Bhimrao Ambedkar University, Lucknow.

☆ Banaras Hindu University, Varanasi.

☆ Bundelkhand University, Jhansi.

☆ B.R. Ambedkar University, Agra.

☆ University of Lucknow, Lucknow.

☆ Mahatma Gandhi Kashi Vidyapeeth, Varanasi.

☆ Mahatma Gandhi Kashi Vidyapeeth, Varanasi.

☆ U.P Rajarshi Tandon Open University, Aollhabad.

☆ Guru Ghasidas University, Bilaspur.

☆ Pandi Ravishankar Shukla University, Raipur.

☆ Andhra University, Vishakapattanam.

☆ Osmania University, Hydrabad.

☆ Sri Krishna devaraya University, Anantpur.

☆ Sri Venkateswara University, Tirupati.

☆ Bangalore University, Banglore.

☆ Gulbarga University, Gulbarga.

☆ Karnatak University, Dharvad.

☆ Kuvempu University, Shimoga.

☆ Mangalore Universiy, Mangalore.

☆ University of Mysore, Mysore.

☆ University of Calicut.

☆ University of Kerela.

☆ Mahatma Gandhi University, Kottayam.

☆ Annamalai University, Annamalainagar.

☆ Bharatidasan University, Tiruchiraplli.

☆ Bishop Heber College, Tiruchiraplli.

☆ Gandhigram Rural Insitute, Gandhigram.

☆ University of Madras, Chennai.

☆ Madurai Kamaraj University, Madurai.

☆ Mother Teresa Womens University, Kodaikenal.

☆ Pondicherry University, Pondicherry.

☆ Birla Institute of Technology, Ranchi.

☆ Lalit Narayan Mithila University, Darbhanga.

☆ Patna University, Patna.

☆ Tilka Manjhi Bhagalpur University, Bhagalpur.

☆ Berhampur University, Ankushpur.

☆ North Orissa University,Sambalpur.

☆ Sambalpur University, Sambalpur.

☆ Utkal University, Bhubaneshwar.

☆ University of Burdwan, Burdwan.

☆ University of Calcutta, Kolkata.

☆ Jadavpur University, Kolkata.

☆ Rabindra Bharati University, Kolkata.

☆ University of Kalyani, Kalyani.

☆ University of North Bengal, Darjeeling.

☆ Vidyasagar University, Midnapore.

☆ Bhavnagar University, Bhavnagar.

☆ Gujarat University, Ahmadabad.

☆ Gujarat Vidyapeth, Ahmadabad.

☆ Hemchandracharya North Gujarat University, Patan.

☆ MS University of Baroda, Vadodara.

☆ Sardar Patel University, Vallabh Vadyanagar.

☆ Saurashtra University, Rajkot.

☆ South Gujarat University, Surat.

☆ Awadesh Pratap Singh University, Rewa.

☆ Barkatullah Vishwavidhyalaya, Bhopal.

☆ Jiwaji University, Gwalior.

☆ D.R. Harisingh Gaur Vishwavidyalaya, Sagar.

☆ Makhanlal Chaturvedi National University, Bhopal.

☆ Rani Durgavati Vishwavidhyalaya, Jabalpur.

☆ Vikram University,Ujjain.

☆ Sant Gadgebaba Amravati University, Amravati.

☆ Bharati Vidhyapeeth, Pune.

☆ Dr. B. A. Marathwada University, Aurangabad.

☆ University of Mumbai, Mumbai.

☆ Rashtrsant Tukdoji Maharaj Nagpur University, Nagpur.

☆ North Maharashtra University, Jalgaon.

☆ University of Pune, Pune.

☆ Shivaji University, Kolhapur.

☆ SNDT Womens University, Mumbai.

☆ Swami Ramanand Teerth Marathwada University, Nanded.

☆ Tilak Maharashtra Vidyapeeth, Pune.

☆ M L Sukhadia University, Udaipur.

☆ University of Rajasthan, Jaipur.

☆ H N B Garhwal University, Srinagar.

☆ Gauhati University, Assam.

☆ Manipur University, Imphal.

☆ North Eastern Hill University, Shilong.

☆ Mizoram University, Aizawl.

☆ Dibrugarh University,

☆ Assam University, Slichar.

LIS Education through Open and Learning Distance

Open and Distance learning has gained momentum over the period of time. The very objective of open and distance learning is to provide access to education. Many open universities and correspondence course institutions in India are offering a number of courses starting from certificate to Ph.D in order to provide higher professional degree.

Objectives

The various objectives associated with this Open University have been mentioned below:

☆ Distance learning can be of vital assistance in overcoming the shortage of qualified personnel,

☆ Provides opportunities for career advancement,

☆ Allows acquiring a higher professional qualification, knowledge and skills,

☆ Acquaints the techniques and management of library systems and services,

☆ Understands the basic functions of each type of library/information center/documentation center in the changing educational and social set up.

☆ Increase awareness and motivation among learners and

☆ Transcends geographical barriers extending access to those in the remote

List of Universities (Distance Mode)

☆ Indira Gandhi National Open University, Delhi.

☆ Dr. B.R. Ambedkar Open University, Hydrabad.

☆ Yashwantrao Chavan Maharashtra Open University, Nashik.

☆ Birla Istitute of Technology and Science, Pilani.

☆ Kaktiya University, Warangal.

☆ Sri Venkatewara University, Tirupati.

☆ Barkhatullah Viswavidyalaya, Bhopal.

☆ Kota Open University, Kota.

☆ University of Calicut, Calicut.

☆ Awdesh pratap singh University, Rewa.

☆ University of Madras

☆ Kurukshetra University, Kurukshetra.

☆ Patna University, Patna.

☆ Guru Ghasidas University,Bilaspur.

☆ Annamalai University, Annamalai.

☆ Alagappa University, Karaikudi.

☆ Bharthidasan University,Tiruchirapalli.

☆ Mahatma Gandhi Gramodaya Viswadyalaya, Chitrakoot.

☆ University of Kashmir, Srinagar.

☆ Madurai Kamraj University, Madurai.

☆ Nalanda Open University, Patna.

☆ Punjabi University,Patiala.

☆ Dr. Hari Singh Gour Viswavidyalaya, Sagar.

☆ Jai Narain Vyas University, Omkarmal Somani College, Jodhpur.

☆ University of Hyderabad, Hydrabad. (PGDLAN)

☆ Lalit Narayan Mithila University, Darbhanga.

☆ M.P.Bhoj University, Bhopal.

Chapter 5

Challenges and Opportunities of e-Collection and Management in Libraries

Electronic Collection : An Introduction

Electronic Collections in a library refer to all those materials which are digital in nature and are stored in different formats in different medium; electronic collection not only include those materials which are stored in computers and storage medium like CD-ROM *etc.*, but also those collections and digital repositories to which the library has license to access. Electronic collections have brought about a sea change in the way in which information has been processed and delivered in the past. Managing electronic collections is different from managing print and other non-digital material for the simple reason that they represent a complex system where content and access are multiple and flexible. Patrons demand for enhanced services as the technology has brought with it the potentiality of 24/7 service and the multi-format of the book content.

Concept of Hybrid Libraries

Hybrid liberaries are mixes of traditional print material such as books and magazines as well as electronic based materials such as electronic journals, ebooks *etc.* The concept of hybrid libraries is generally understood as a development towards fully digital library; however fully digital library is yet to be as it implies not only a technology shift but most importantly a cultural shift (Oppenheim, 1999). This is true especially as far as Indian scenario is concerned, because the term library generally means premises which has readable collections and is located in a place.

A hybrid library consists of both print material and a growing number of electronic sources. What we are presently concerned is the impact of the growing electronic material available both under open access and under purchase in the collection management of the libraries. Just as Information and Communication Technology has influenced banking, education and other sectors, libraries have also been over the past few decades adopted new technologies to improve the overall function and management of the library. Managing electronic collections in a hybrid library calls for an efficient integration of digital materials with the physical space.

Major Issues Related to Electronic Collections

Traditional Material vs Digital Resources

Electronic resources bring with them certain new issues like authentication, access, usage, administration, networking, pricing, technology standards and much more. From the perspective of collection management, some important issues are as follows:

1. Selection and Acquisition

Electronic collections come with certain complex problems regarding access, networking, pricing, licensing, ownership and last but not the least, rapidly changing technology and technology standards. With electronic resources the selector cannot make a decision to acquire an electronic resource in isolation and must liaise closely with other departments in the library and other departments to evaluate the suitability of a resource prior to the decision to acquire.

2. License and Access Agreements

The materials collected are not in physical form and hence the limitations are placed on the licensee's ability to transfer the acquired materials to the third parties. Electronic information is not physically packed; it is transmitted electronically from publisher to the purchaser or licensee. This brings with it a range of access options which result in a variety of pricing models. Whatever be the terms and conditions most of the commercial vendors of information, under most licenses either restrict or do not allow universal access.

3. Technical Issues

Technical considerations include the various aspects of maintaining and accessing various digital collections and integrating them into a proper system to serve the users. It includes issues like remote access (i.e in a network) or stand alone access, mode of access to the digital collection like availability through IP filtering or password based access, hardware and software maintenance, storage issues which include local hosting and remote hosting, suitable platforms which facilitate access to e- resources.

Some important technical issues are summarized as under:

☆ **Compatibility:** The existing hardware and software in the library should support the electronic resources and more importantly, the electronic resources should be compatible across a range of platforms. In those cases where there is local installation and maintenance, additional requirements regarding software, hardware and multimedia components have to be taken care of with regard to the existing system.

☆ **Authentication:** It is two types namely, IP based or password based. In the case of IP based access, which is used within the physical confines of the institution, the facility could be extended outside the campus using a proxy server. If the access is password based, it presents some challenges in the dissemination of information and password control and hence it is better to insist on a disclaimer in the license agreement that the library cannot have a control over the password distribution to non-affiliates.

☆ **Content:** The e-content comes in various formats. Databases containing multimedia files like audio and video files require different programs to be installed and the necessary plug-ins and active controls have to be allowed for accessing those files.

In selecting an electronic resource or a database we have to consider the following aspects of the resource.

☆ **User Friendly interface**: An interface well designed ensures the optimum use of the content available in the database. The screen should be simple, easy to follow.

☆ **Search and Retrieval**: The electronic resource should offer a robust search engine which is capable of handling transliteration and include features like Boolean search, keyword search and full-text search, truncation, browsing, thesaurus, search history *etc.*

☆ **Availability:** The system should be available throughout with good networking facility and up-to-date technology to support maximum number of users.

☆ **Download facility:** The system should support exporting and downloading required files and mailing them; citation management software (like Endnote, BibTex *etc.* should be available.

☆ **Electronic Information Delivery**: This is a variation of the Selective Dissemination of Information; User profiles are automatically collected through their information search pattern and their areas of interest.

☆ **Electronic Reference:** Electronic reference has brought new dimensions to the already existing library reference services. E-mail, chat and instant messaging through social networks have added value to the already existing one –to –one response between the librarian and patron. Apart from these there are also other impersonal online services like FAQs, Virtual reference desks, Pathfinders *etc.*

Adapting Innovative Technology in Library Practices

New forms of information sources and collections come as new technology innovations are coming up in the market. Librarians have been quick to adopt these tools and exploit them to the benefit of the libraries in which they serve. The decision to go electronic triggers an entirely new way of organizing the library materials and also the way in which the information is delivered.

1. Library Management – New Emerging Trends

Change here comes from the management level and it may be a result of takeover or mergers *etc*. In the case of a library, it may be reforms on the library policies and any major change in budgeting and other changes which are initiated at the management level. The role of library has changed to that of an information centre, where there is a huge dependence on online and digital resources.

2. Process Change and Adopting Innovative Technology

There has been rapid change in the past two decades in computer technology and particularly database management systems and networking technology. Information and communication technology is the buzzword and this has opened up a plethora of opportunities in the field of library and information science. Librarian has varied options in managing the library and introducing innovative services and facilities in his library. The users and the staff also have to be initiated into new services and technology that is being introduced into the library system. This needs a lot of initiative on the part of the librarian to educate and orient the staff and users of the library. Especially in case of introducing certain facilities which are technology dependent like internet resources, e-books, CD databases and OPAC, there is a need for user orientation and the user has to be enlightened on all these aspects. Similarly, the users also have to be acquainted with the security systems like RFID *etc.*

3. Squeeze in Expenditure and Resource Sharing through Consortia

Cost cutting has been a recurrent change which almost every librarian has been facing and he has to effectively manage the cost squeeze from operations by not abruptly cutting down certain facilities in the library. Consortia effort has been a boon in the given situation.

4. Literacy Programs Information

Information literacy programmes, user orientation and staff training on a regular basis helps the librarian to manage the situation as and when new systems and practices are being implemented in the library.

5. Change in the Attitude of the Staff

This deals purely with the psychological reaction of the staff and users in the library. Any change in the system should not cause any feeling of insecurity among the staff. Likewise users also should not feel alienated and the atmosphere should not turn hostile due to certain changes brought about. Hence any change should be well planned and efficiently executed and the feedback after the change has been implemented should be obtained for further improvement.

Digital Resources Management: Some Problems

Digital resources bring some problems which are unique to them. There are some problems, right from acquiring those collections up to dissemination of the digital resources.

1. Digital Divide is an Impotant Issue

The gap could be narrowed by giving proper training to the staff and orientation and user education to the users in making use of the electronic resources.

2. Heterogeneous Information Resources

Many of the resources are hidden and the regular search tools do not provide access to the deep web or the hidden web. Federated search tools are being used to search information across different databases and repositories but still they have their own limitations; one of them being licenses of certain database providers may not allow the inclusion of their databases.

3. Electronic Access License Agreement

Electronic access agreements authorize to access the content under a given set of conditions. The limitations may be temporal or restricting the number of users over a particular period of time. There are different pricing models available which makes the librarian's choice difficult. Sometimes there is little control over the contractual obligations as the terms of liability are not known at the time of placing order (Gopal, 2000). However, many national and international associations have developed guidance to help information managers negotiate licenses or to better understand their implications for libraries and other users.

4. Information Security in a Liberary

Information security in a library would include personnel security and policies, steps taken for effective backups, and the physical integrity of computing facilities, effective maintenance and security of digital resources, network security *etc.*The security measures that could be possibly taken by a library are a complete audit of software and hardware is performed for each computer and it is ensured that there are no unnecessary components like additional software *etc.* Use of network switches in the place of hubs to prevent packet switching in those cases where the software on the computers is subject to change, by either accident or malicious intent, the computer software could be refreshed from a LAN server at every reboot or perform nightly backups to spot inconsistencies and flag problems. User rights and the level of access should be well defined.

5. Archiving Policy

Unlike print publications, electronic publications may not be maintained on a permanent basis. It is important to consider the effect of cancellation of an agreement on the previously acquired content.

6. Library Budgets Problem

This is common problem to both traditional as well as digital collections. But unlike non-digital materials, there is no standard pricing model for electronic collections and the librarian has to use his discretion in choosing the materials and negotiating the terms of license with the vendor.

General Skill of Librarian for Electronic Collections

- ☆ Realize the value of distributed services and recognize the potential of sharing the resources in a digitized networked environment.
- ☆ Assessment of user needs and identify the collections.
- ☆ Understanding the pattern of information flow - *i.e.* how it is created, evaluated, organized disseminated and used.
- ☆ Leverage staff knowledge and skills.
- ☆ Ensure interoperability by creating crosswalks or harvesting protocols as needed.
- ☆ Develop application profile(s).
- ☆ Understanding the various methods and principles of organization of information and appreciate the role of cataloging and metadata in information organization.
- ☆ Choosing Metadata standard, content standard and leverage existing metadata.
- ☆ Knowledge of international standards and a good understanding of at least two schemas with their advantages and limitations.
- ☆ Determine the infrastructure required, *i.e.* Selection of hardware and Software required.
- ☆ Create template for data input.
- ☆ Develop work flow.

Chapter 6

Use of e-Resources: A Boon to User of Academic Libraries

Electronic Resources

An e-resource is defined as an information resource which is in an electronic format requiring computer network for accessing. This type of resources includes e-journals, images, multimedia products, e-books and other information resources in electronic form *etc*. The E- Resources may be accessed on CDs, tapes, via internet and so on. In modern libraries E-Resources are being proved as more effective tools in satisfying the information needs of the users.

Category of e-Resources

The e-resources are basically categorized in two types:

I. Online e-Resources, Which may Include:

1. e-journal (Full text and bibliographic database)
2. e-books
3. on-line databases
4. Web sites

II. Other Electronic Resources

1. PCD ROM
2. Diskettes
3. Other portable computer databases *etc*.

Advantages of e-Resources

The reasons for actually embarking on the purchasing of electronic resources are generally accepted because of the ease of usability, readability, affordability and accessibility. The following are the advantages of e-resources over the print media:

1. **Multi-access:** A networked product can provide multiple points of access in time (24 hours a day. 7 days a week) and to multiple simultaneous users.

2. **Speed:** An electronic resource is lot quicker to browse or search, to extract information from, and to integrate that information into other material and to cross-search or reference between different publications.

3. **Functionality:** E-resource will allow the user to approach the publications to analyze its content in new ways by click of the mouse on search mode.

4. **Content:** The e- resources can contain a vast amount of information, but more importantly the material can consist of mixed media *i.e.* images, video, audio animation which could not be replaced in print.

5. **Other advantages of e-resources may include:** international reach, unlimited capabilities, reduced cost, convenience, search ability and linking.

Library Network (Inflibnet)

INFLIBNET emerged as a front runner, facilitates automation and networking of academic libraries for resource sharing. INFLIBNET's beginning was made in 1991 as a major programme of UGC under the Inter-University Centre for Astronomy and Astrophysics (IUCAA). The INFLIBNET Centre was established in May 1996 as an independent, autonomous Inter-University Centre (IUC) of the University Grants commission (UGC) in Ahmedabad, India with the target to network all the academic libraries of higher education in India. The main activities and services of this centre include automation of academic libraries and information centres, creation of union databases of resources of academic libraries, promotion of resource sharing among academic libraries, promotion of information access and transfer, supporting scholarship, learning and academic pursuits *etc.*

Library Consortium

A library consortium is a network of Libraries/Information Centres that agree for resource sharing in order to satisfy the information needs of users on the basis of library cooperation.

Reason for Information of Consortia

1. Better sharing of existing resources and jointly acquiring new resources at great savings

2. Expediting inter library borrowing, which has evolved into providing as many electronic resources as possible at the lowest cost to consortia members.

3. Providing enhanced library services with an emphasis on access to new electronic resources including databases and services offered through the internet and the WWW.

Consortium at International Level

Consortium of University Research Libraries (CURL), The British Columbia Electronic Library Network (ELN), Texas State Electronic Library Consortium of Academic Libraries in Manchester; Colorado Library Information Network and Washington Research Library Consortium and Library Consortia in Oregon, Washington and Idaho, GALILIO, Ohiolink, Texshare, VIVA and SUNYConnect in USA; CONCERT in Taiwan; CALIS in China.

Consortium at National Level

UGC-INFONET Digital Library Consortium, Indian National Digital Library in Engineering, Science and Technology (INDEST) Consortium, Inter-University Centres (IUC-DAEF) Consortia for Atomic Energy, FORSA (Forum for Resource Sharing in Astronomy and Astrophysics, CSIR-Journal Consortium, HELINET (Health Science Library and Information Network), Ce-RA (Consortium for e-Resources in Agriculture).

Ugc-Infonet Digital Library Consortium

The UGC-INFONET Digital Library Consortium is major initiative of UGC to bring qualitative change in academic world in India. It was formally launched in December 2003 by Honorable Dr. A.P.J. Abdul Kalam, the then President of India, soon after providing the Internet connectivity to the Universities in the year 2003 under the UGC-INFONET programme. This consortium is an ambitious programme for providing access to scholarly electronic resources including full-text and bibliographical databases in all subject disciplines to academic and research community in India in order to bring qualitative change in teaching, learning and research in Indian higher education.

Aims and Objectives of the UGC-Infonet Digital Library Consortium

The major aims and objectives of this consortium are as under:

1. To provide access to a high-quality and scholarly electronic resource to a large number of academic institution including universities and colleges at substantially lower rates of subscription and at most favourable terms and conditions;
2. To extend the benefit of consortium to its associate members including private universities and colleges;
3. To promote rapid and efficient access to scholarly content to the users and to create and promote use of ICT in teaching and learning in universities in India;

4. To impart training to the users, librarians, research scholars and faculty members of the institutions in use of electronic resources with an aim to optimize their usage;

5. To evaluate the usage of the subscribed resources and to identify new resources that are required to be subscribed under the programme;

6. To increase the research productivity of the institution both in terms of quality and quantity of publication.

7. To promote use of e-resources with gradual decrease in print subscription; To promote interaction and inter-library co-operation amongst the participating universities;

8. To bring qualitative change in teaching, learning and research with an aim to meet the ever growing challenges of globalization of higher education and it acts as a single-window service for a big number of academic institutions, with their vivid research and academic interests in India. This consortium makes available e-resources to participating institutions at highly discounted rates of subscription with most favorable terms and conditions of agreements. The rates offered to the consortium are lower by 60 per cent to 99 per cent depending upon the category of institutions.

Major Activities of the Consortium

1. To measure usage of existing e-resources and its impact of research output in terms of number of research publications;

2. To arrange subscription to electronic resources identified and negotiated by the members of its National Steering Committee;

3. Encourage interactions amongst member Libraries.

4. Interact with the officials in UGC for continuation and promotion of the programme;

5. Organize training programmes for the member institutions on use of electronic resources;

6. Ensure access to subscribed electronic resources to member universities as per their subscription;

7. Interact with ERNET (now BSNL) India for providing uninterrupted Internet bandwidth in the member universities; Initiate additional activities complementary to the present activities of the Consortium and;

8. To identify new resources relevant to the user community in universities;

9. Interaction with member Libraries to ensure optimal utilization of subscribed electronic resources;

Consortium has currently following types of members:

1. Universities under Purview of UGC (Core Members)

All Universities covered under 12B of UGC Act are entitled to be the member of the Consortium. These Universities are considered as core members. All expenses on subscription to e-resources for these universities are borne by the UGC. As per the diversity of resources needed and ICT infrastructure available in these universities, 182 universities currently covered under the programme.

2. Associate Members

The Associate Membership programme for the UGC-INFONET Digital Library Consortium has recently been introduced wherein e-resources subscribed by the Consortium are made available on subscription to private universities and other academic institutions at low rates of subscription and favorable terms and conditions of subscription.

3. College Model of the Consortium

There is also a proposal to extend services of this Consortium to Colleges with Potential for Excellence (CPE) as well as to autonomous colleges having adequate ICT infrastructure. Besides, the INFLIBNET Centre is also actively working closely with MHRD to extend the services of the Consortium to all its affiliated colleges under the National Mission on Education through ICT. The proposal named "National Library and Information Services Infrastructure for Scholarly Content" (N-LIST) is being evolved in collaboration with the UGC-INFONET Digital Library Consortium and the INDEST-AICTE Consortium.

e-Resources Subscribed by the UGC-INFONET Digital Library Consortium

e-Resources	URL
Full-text Resources	
American Chemical Society	http://www.pubs.acs.org/
American Institute of Physics	http://journals.aip.org/
American Physical Society	http://publish.aps.org/browse.php
Annual Reviews	http://arjournals.annualreviews.org/
Wiley-Blackwell Publishing	http://www3.interscience.wiley.com/
Cambridge University Press	http://journals.cambridge.org/
Economic and Political Weekly	http://www.epw.in/
Elsevier Science	http://www.sciencedirect.com/
Emerald	http://iris.emeraldinsight.com/
Institute of Physics	http://www.iop.org/EJ/
Jstor	http://www.jstor.org/
Nature	http://www.nature.com/nature/
Oxford University Press	http://www.oxfordjournals.org
Portland Press	http://www.portlandpress.com/pp/Journals/default.htm
Project Euclid	http://projecteuclid.org/
Project Muse	http://muse.jhu.edu/journals
Royal Society of Chemistry	http://www.rsc.org/Publishing/Journals/

e-Resources	URL
SIAM	http://epubs.siam.org/
Springer Link	http://www.springerlink.com/
Taylor and Francis	http://informaworld.com/
Heinonline	http://home.heinonline.org/
Manupatra	http://www.manupatra.com/
Westlaw India	http://www.westlawindia.com
Bibliographic Databases	
JCCC	http://jccc-infonet.informindia.co.in
MathSciNet	http://www.ams.org/mathscinet
SciFinderScholar	http://www.cas.org/SCIFINDER/SCHOLAR/index.html
ISID	http://isid.org.in
Royal Society of Chemistry	http://www.rsc.org/publishing/CurrentAwareness/
(6 Databases)	index.asp
Web of Science	http://isiknowledge.com/
(Through N-LIST Programme)	
Open Access Resources	http://www.oaresources.php

Using e-Resources

The access to e-resources is IP-enabled for the member universities/institutions. As such a user does not need "Login ID and Password" to access resources available to his/her institution, in stead, the resources are accessible to them across the campus network. The Consortium also maintains a website (http://www.inflibnet.ac.in/econ/). Creating awareness about access to e-resources among participating members is very necessary in order to make the maximum benefit of the Consortium. The INFLIBNET Centre organizes "One-Day User Awareness Programme" and "Two-Days User Awareness Programme" at participating Universities/Institution. Till now more than 62 such programmes have been organized. Considering the actual demand of the user's community, the consortium has proposal to add more e-resources to its list including electronic books, full-text journals and bibliographic databases, datasets and reference books *etc*.

Chapter 7

Electronic Books: An Ecofriendly Learning Tool

An Overview

It is well known that e-resources are the trend of the later part of the 20th century and came in the wake of advances in computer and communication technologies. Now, with the emergence of these resources the text and data is available online and is read on the end user's computer which is significantly different from publishing in print on the paper. It is in the digital form and does not require any intermediary medium. Information is directly accessed from the host computer. E-resources are "Material consisting of data and/or computer program(s) encoded for reading and manipulation by a computer by the use of a peripheral device directly connected to the computer or remotely via a network. The category includes software application, electronic text, bibliographic databases, *etc.*

Along with different types of e-resources, E-books are also becoming popular among the youngsters of I.T. era due to their various advantages. But they are still not comfortable to all the readers. There may be several issues behind this non preference. "Dr Ramaiah's article provides an overview of users' perception about e-books in India. Though the Indian readers are aware of the advantages and limitations of e-books, they continue to prefer and use printed publications. Usage of electronic books is one of the important aspects for developing collections in the university libraries. The pages viewed, pages copied, pages printed, unique documents usage, and user sessions were identified to determine the extent of usage in academic institutions. Kaba and Dr Raed Said provide the results of usage reports for ebrary database in the UAE. They found that a large number of institutions do not optimally use ebrary services so in-house training programmes are essential to improve their usage" (Ramaiah, 2012, Desidoc).

Concept of e-Books

In 1945, Vannevar Bush for the first time mentioned about the concept of e-book in his seminal article *'As we may think'* published in *The Atlantic Monthly*. In that article, Bush described about the 'memex' a conceptual mechanical device used to store, retrieve, and display personal books, records, and documents. Taking this idea, Andries van Dam, a computer science professor at Brown University, has developed several models and interfaces for the e-books during the last three decades. Almost at the same time, Alan Kay developed the Dynabook, which is similar to today's laptop computer. Under Project Gutenberg project, on 4 July 1971, Michael Hart first time created 'Declaration of Independence' a digital book and sent it to many people over a network.

After Internet became popular in1990s, some publishers started publishing and selling e-books along with their print versions. With the launch of NetLibrary by OCLC in 1999, about 2,000 e-books became commercially available to libraries. Later, e-book providing companies Questia and ebrary, entered into the market with different access models in 2000. Both of them marketed their services directly to end-users and also promoted institutional accounts to librarians, with mixed results" (Chennupati K. Ramaiah, DJLIT, 2012). The first e-book proudly raised its head in 1971 with Project Gutenberg. For libraries, their proliferation began in 1998 with the launch of NetLibrary.

Definitions of Electronic Book

According to new Concise Oxford English Dictionary (2001) "e-book is 'an electronic version of a printed book which can be read on a personal computer or handheld device designed specifically for this purpose". According to Ormes (2000) "the term e-book is used specifically to describe a text which requires the use of e-book software or hardware to read'. She notes, however, that the term can also refer to the hand-held device used to read the texts" (quoted in Lee, 2002). Chennupati K. Ramaiah, 2012 says "An e-book is nothing but a computer file/electronic copy of printed book that needs a device such as PC or PDA or web, to access and read".

Definition by Armstrong, Edwards and Lonsdale (2002) represents better the term. According to them "any piece of electronic text regardless of size or composition (a digital object), but excluding journal publications, made available electronically (or optically) for any device (handheld or desk-bound) that includes a screen".

Formats of e-Books

Divakar (2012) has categorized e-books into three following types on the basis of their content formats:

- ☆ **HTML e-book**: This type of e-books are created using the hypertext markup language. It is like the web pages are created and compiled into compressed executable file.
- ☆ **Document e-book**: These types of e-books are first created into the format of word processor. After completion of the document in word processor

it is simply converted into pdf file with.pdf extension by using software required namely Adobe Acrobat Reader.

☆ **Handheld e-book:** These are compatible with using handheld e-book reader. A number of such readers are available in market.

Accessing of an e-Book

According to Lee (2002) there are five ways of accessing an e-Book

☆ **Online via web:** E-book may be accessed via a standard web browser. The web interface allows user to read the text and it also provides the facility of linking to other resources. NetLibrary and Questia are such companies which offer web access to e-books.

☆ **Downloading to a PC (or Mac):** In this method, a user may download e-book on his/her PC from internet with dedicated piece of software like adobe's acrobat reader.

☆ **Downloading to hand held readers:** In this method, a user may read e-book through such e-readers.

☆ **Downloading to e-book specific devices:** There are specific pieces of hardware which may be used for reading e-books. These devices are having many special feautures like larger screens and better interfaces, light in weight, portable, good storage capacity, extensive battery life, and many other additional features.

☆ **Print on paper:** Many users are fond of reading e-books in print format Thus many services offer the user the option of sending paper copy hence this way is called Print On Demand (POD). A few companies like InstBooks, ODMS, sprout and NetLibrary provide such service.

e-Book Providers and Platform

The reader can download and save a number of e-books "from a variety of sources, including online e-book stores, like Amazon.com or Barnes and Noble, literary sites, and even public domain titles in EPUB and PDF form, as well as older Sony e-bookstore titles through Adobe Digital Editions (ADE) DRM scheme Today the major e-book distribution channels in the world include Amazon.com, publishers' e-commerce sites, Barnes and Noble e-books store, Apple iBookstore, Kobo, Borders, Sony e-books store, *etc.* However, Amazon has greater share among these on e-book reading devices and e-books over others. It is noticed that 85 per cent of publishers produce books both in print and electronic version and only about 10 per cent of publishers, e-books alone. Other devices have a seemingly vast (600,000+ titles), but very proprietary list to download from and must have Wi-Fi capability from which they should connect.

Issues Related to e-Books

It is indubitable that E-books are imperative component of IT based e-resources but still their growth depends upon the perceptions of different people involved.

For this specific collections' growth, mainly the users, libraries, publishers, vendors and authors and their viewpoints are involved.

I. Users (Readers)

Literature regarding the use of e-books reveals that more users still preferred printed books instead of e-books. There are many reasons such as- high price, portability, flexibility, lack of hardware and software knowledge, quality of content, clarity of the screen definition and inability to read graphs, charts and pictures in e-books, non- availability in libraries, *etc.*

II. Publishers and Vendors

Publishers and vendors have their own vital role to promote e-book collection in libraries. If publishers or vendors develop a few methods of providing unrestricted access and provide surety for long life access/perpetual access of e-books, it can promote different libraries to subscribe the same.

III. Authors/Writers

Like majority of existing e-journals are based on their print counterpart, majority of e-books are not produced/born digital rather they are electronic or digital versions of their print format. "Authors therefore need to use different techniques for developing born digital e-books. Authors/Writers are obviously responsible for the intellectual content of the ebook. Also, as with p-books, determining who is the copyright holder and how monies accrued from sales/licensing of e-books are to be apportioned between author and publishers needs to be addressed" (Tedd, 2005). Besides some authors are happy for conversion of their intellectual content into e-format by publishers while others are not receptive for this and refused it. This is all because of e- publishing and electronic rights deals.

Libraries and e-Books

Libraries will mainly prefer to make its part of that collection type which is commonly or mostly used by its user community. The subscription of this particular type of collection also depends on the allocated budget to the libraries for their collection. "Libraries have tight budget so it is important that the resources they buy are justifiable and well used by its clientele. For libraries it's not the "one time" purchases, but to continue to fund annual access fees also. Inspite of this, librarians should understand that whatever purchase models they propose for purchase of e-books, it must accommodate the commercial viability of the publishers also" (Rakesh Mani Sharma, 2012, AALDI). Besides, there comes problems of cataloguing of this collection and integration with other resources of library.

Chapter 8

Electronic Resources in Higher Education Libraries and its Familiarity

An Overview

The Higher Education Academic libraries endeavor to offer of information knowledge services according to the needs of its library users. Towards this objective, they put together a collection of information resources. The advances in information and communication system have opened up the possibility of instant access and dissemination of information as it is created. The electronic library or digital library is the product of the technological expansion which enriched the field of library and information systems. The accessories we utilize in these libraries are CD-ROM, DVD, floppy disks, multimedia, computers, *etc.*, and now the internet. The information technology, especially the internet has profoundly changed the ways of publication. Now a day's news paper, magazines and periodicals are getting published online versions and all kinds of texts are now available in digitized form. Publications are appearing with mixed media and they are in electronic format. Digital media and networks have created new products in the network society. Dissemination of information is changing with the increasing importance of computer technology.

Various Format of Electronic Resources

Various formats such as E-books-journals, online databases, CD-ROMs, reference sources, etc are found in liberary resources. We found that the uses of e-journals are very popular in academic and research institutions. The other web resources like the online databases are also used in various libraries. However the printed books are not replaced with e-books as compared with e-journals. There are several reasons like technological limitations, tendency of user, and financial limitations *etc.* The two types of e-resources are classified as formal and informal.

1. Formal Electronic Resources

☆ **Indexing and abstracting databases:** A large number of indexing and abstracting information services of the world have created their own databases, which can be searched from any part of the world on payment basis to retrieve necessary information.

☆ **Full-text databases:** These resources provide full- text of the document apart from its bibliographical information. Nowadays various publishers are providing access to full text/databases through the internet. *e.g.* American Chemical Society.

☆ **On-line:** Online journals are defined as those that are available on "Pay-as-you go" or 'cost per access basis' via such online hosts. These e-journals are not considered as a part of library collection, because most of the library users are rarely allowed free or unlimited access to the remote online system. Basically, online journals are the electronic version of existing printed journals, *e.g.*; American Chemical Society.

☆ **e-journals-licensed or open access:** e-journal is one which is available in electronic form and can be accessed using computer and communication technologies. It is published and distributed in electronic media. Publisher/Aggregator charging some fee to access the resources are called paid or licensed resources. Some publishers are providing free access to few of their journals and many organizations are making open access to their products. The e-journals are classified to in three types.

☆ **Networked journals:** With the emergence of the internet, revolution took place in the periodicals publication sector. Now major publishers are using the internet as a medium to publish and the web as a global way for making their publications available to all. Mostly e-journals are available as databases where number of e-journals are available together.

☆ **CD-ROM :** These are full text journals published and distributed in the form of CD-ROM at a particular frequency along with search software to access and print. Number of publishers have started publishing some of their core journals in CD-ROM form during the last couples of years.

☆ **e-books-licensed or open access:** E-books is electronic version of books, delivered to readers in digital formats. They can be read on all types of computers. Including hand held devices designed specifically for reading e-books.

☆ **Numeric and statistical databases:** It provides historical, financial, statistical and marketing information.

☆ **Reference databases:** Publishers are providing users with various reference sources through their websites and databases, such as dictionaries, yearbooks, encyclopedias, *etc.*

★ **Multimedia products:** Multimedia products are finding profound use in education and training. In class room lectures operation of a machine, a particular experimentation in a laboratory, a surgery in an operation theatre, *etc.* For using these products a well-configured computer system is needed.

2. Informal Electronic Resources

★ **Blogs:** Blog is an online diary where one can post information (not only text but also audio, photographs and videos) on a regular basis. Blog defined as referring content management (or distribution) tool/system that helps to broadcast useful information to end-user, in order to promote and create awareness in electronic environment.

★ **E-mail:** User sends the library an e-mail with a reference query, requesting to supply whatever information he or she feels is necessary. The library may reply by e-mails, phone, fax, letter, *etc.* Now a days the Web pages of libraries are coming with "Ask a Librarian "option.

Advantages

Most electronic resources come equipped with powerful search-and-retrieval tools that allow users to perform literature searches more efficiently and effectively than was previously possible.

★ Electronic resources are available to users and they can access them 24 hours a day through the Web.

★ Navigate directly from indexing databases to the full text of an article and even follow further links from there.

★ The user can re-specify his or her needs dynamically.

★ The information is obtained based on the need so becomes "just in time" rather than "just in case".

★ Electronic information can therefore provide a number of advantages over traditional print based sources.

Chapter 9

e-Technology: A Golden Opportunity for Farmers

An Introduction

Although Indian economy is based on agriculture, the interest shown by farmers is very meagre owing to less quantity of agricultural products in comparison to their expenditure. Consequently, the young generation in the rural areas, move to urban places in search of white collar jobs. But today, the scenario is different in agriculture sector with the onset and application of e-technology like smart phone.

Technologies like remote sensing and computer simulation help to assess speed and direction of wind, soil quality and recommendations, crop yield predictions. It provides information to farmers on seeds, fertilizers, pesticides, weather, marketing of agricultural products and various government schemes like Kisan Credit Card. In addition, it helps the farmers in improved decision making, better planning, sharing innovative techniques and community involvement. Through this e-technology, the farmers will get detailed and well monitored report on weather, soil, fertilizers, quality of crops, agricultural prices, *etc.* It helps them to obtain pertinent information immediately. It also highlights various Information Communication Technologies (ICTs) through social media tools like Facebook, Twitter, YouTube, Whatsapp, etc

Impact of e-Technology

Due to technological developments, farmers can access farming materials available around the world through web based services. In spite of ICT advancements, communication has definitely been made easier through these new technological developments, but the concern is how far they are helpful in making agriculture more distinct in the economy and GDP of developing countries.

e-Technology in Farming: Agriculture in India is the core sector in the economy of our country. At present, ICT has a main role in the growth of Indian agriculture. The technology props in the correct choice of fertilizers and pesticides. Selling and buying of agricultural products online has become popular in India.ICTs and applications have a great potential for agricultural extension.

e-Governance is another example of this technology. Practice of e-governance creates transparency which enable the people to a great extent. It helps to maintain land records by removing the malpractices and creating assurance of rightful ownership of land.

DD Kisan is an Indian agriculture 24-hour television channel, which is owned by Doordarshan and was launched on 26th May 2015. The channel is dedicated to agriculture and allied sectors, which disseminates real-time inputs to farmers on new farming techniques, water conservation and organic farming among other information. Through social media like facebook and whatsApp, farmers can contact other farmers, scientists and experts in other regions. Smart phones are more convenient, affordable and accessible to connect to facebook than computers. Agriculture is transforming with the use of technologies that allow farmers to connect to each other and share information.

Twitter: It is seen as a prime place for professional networking for news and updates, and for use as a back channel in conferences and for real time chats.

YouTube: This is a video hosting site which is both a key learning resource and a place for anyone to share their own video content.

WhatsApp: It is not just as a popular personal messaging app, but its broadcasting and group functionalities make it a valuable tool both for educational and corporate activities.

Facebook: It is one of the most popular social network sites among researchers and farmers in India for sharing of information.

The application of Information and Communications Technology (ICT) in agriculture is increasingly important. ICTs such as e -mail, mobile phones, and Internet among others are required for effective extension information among farmers. Social networking websites like Facebook, Twitter, Google+, Whatsapp, Linkedin, Flickr, *etc.* are also used for dissemination of agricultural research and innovative information to the extension workers and farmers. Many online free apps are available for farmers for their agricultural operations.

e-Agriculture is an emerging field focusing on the enhancement of agricultural and rural development through improved information and communication processes. More specifically, e-Agriculture involves the conceptualization, design, development, evaluation and application of innovative ways to use ICT in the rural domain, with a primary focus on agriculture.

All stakeholders of agriculture industry need information and knowledge about crop cultivation, water management, fertilizer application, irrigation, pest management, harvesting, post-harvest handling, transport of food products, packaging, food preservation, food processing, quality management, food safety, food storage, and food marketing to manage them efficiently. Any system applied for getting information and knowledge for making decisions in any industry should deliver accurate, complete, concise information in time. The information provided by the system must be in user-friendly form, easy to access, cost-effective and well protected from unauthorized accesses.

Smartphone Mobile Apps in Agriculture

Use of mobile technologies as a tool of intervention in agriculture is increasingly popular. Reach of smart phone even in rural areas extended the ICT services beyond simple voice or text messages. Several smartphone apps are available for agriculture, horticulture, animal husbandry and farm machinery.

Satellite Farming

It is a farming management concept based on observing, measuring and responding to inter and intra-field variability in crops. This technique focuses on utilizing resources optimally to improve the quality and quantity of crops while lowering the cost of production. It reduces fertilizer and pesticide use, prevents soil degradation, utilizes water optimally and raises productivity. Globally, this is done with the aid of modern, eco-friendly farming practices and technology, including satellite imagery and information technology. The applications of nano-technology will help in improving fertilizer, water use efficiency and exploiting the benefits of precision agriculture.

Geographic Information Systems (GIS)

GIS are extensively used in agriculture, especially in precision farming. Land is mapped digitally, and pertinent geodetic data such as topography and contours are combined with other statistical data for easier analysis of the soil. GIS is used in decision making such as what to plant and where to plant using historical data and sampling.

Global Positioning System (GPS)

In agriculture, the use of the Global Positioning System provides benefits in map-making and surveying. With the use of GPS, civilians can produce simple yet highly accurate digitized map without the help of a professional cartographer. It helps the farmers about the quantity of fertilizers to be used, and also about yield, moisture, drainage, *etc.*

The technology of remote sensing, GIS and GPS is continuously evolving with improvement in satellite data resolution and increased availability of multitemporal data and will be able to address emerging challenges in developing resource inventory and monitoring land use planning. The assessment and mapping of soil moisture availability in time and space plays a pivotal role in crop planning. The potential of remotely sensed microwave data needs to be tapped for the same.

Webcams help farmers to monitor the crops and to take the expertise from the scientists to address the problems faced by the farmers without taking the scientists to the field.

The Kisan Call Centre Scheme is functioning since 21st January 2004 with a specific purpose for effective use of delivering knowledge and information to the farming community. The Kisan Call Centers can be accessed by farmers all over the country on common Toll Free Number 1551 from land line telephone and 1800-180-1551 from any mobile phone to seek expert advice on different matters pertaining to agriculture and allied sectors. This system also helps to keep a record of what is being delivered to the farmers in terms of knowledge and information.

Kisan SMS Portal: Here farmers keep getting SMS messages providing information or delivering service or giving advices on their mobiles from experts, scientists and officers at various level after opting for messages on agricultural practices or crops of their interest. Messages are customized based on farmer's preferences in the language chosen by them. They can register themselves by calling the Kisan call centre on the toll free number or through web portal or even SMS.

Kisan Credit Card: It uses the ICT to provide affordable credit for farmers in India. It was started by the Government of India, Reserve Bank of India (RBI), and National Bank for Agriculture and Rural Development (NABARD) in 1998-99 to help farmers access timely and adequate credit.

The Kisan Credit Card allows farmers to have cash credit facilities without going through time-consuming bank credit screening processes repeatedly. Repayment can be rescheduled if there is a bad crop season, and extensions are offered for upto four years. The card is valid for three years and subject to annual renewals.

Soil Health Card (SHC)

The Central Government launched the Soil Health Card Scheme in February 2015. Under this programme, the government plans to issue soil card to farmers to help them get better yield by studying the quality of soil, and other functional characteristics like water and nutrients content, other biological properties and corrective measures. The farmers use fertilisers and pesticides (even in large quantity) without knowing the quality of their land, and thus, end up damaging the land's fertility and wasting fertiliser and pesticide. With the help of the Soil Health Card, farmers come to know about the quantity of these to be used for their soil and crop suitability.

According to the scheme, the objective is to issue the soil cards to farmers spread all over India. Following are the ways by which farmers are helped by this card:

- ☆ With the issue of the card, the farmers will get a well-monitored report of the soil which is chosen for cultivation of crops.
- ☆ The monitoring will be done on a regular basis.
- ☆ The farmers will be guided by experts to come up with solutions to improve the quality of the soil.
- ☆ Regular monitoring will help the farmers to get a long-term soil health record and accordingly can study and evaluate the results of different soil management practices.

☆ This card can become most helpful and effective when filled out regularly by the same person over a period of time.

☆ The idea is not to compare the varied soil types but to find out methods to improve soil fertility, to access the different types of soil and their ability to support crop production in spite of their limitations and as per their abilities.

☆ The soil card will help the farmers to get an idea on the crop-wise recommendations of nutrients and fertilizers required in each type of soil. This can help in increasing the crop yield.

In order to make the scheme more successful, the government of India, along with the agriculture department of India, has launched a soil health card agriculture portal. The farmers need to register at the web portal www.soilhealth.dac.gov.in along with the details of the soil samples and test lab reports. Thereafter the experts will analyse the strength and weaknesses of the soil and suggest measures to deal with it. The result and suggestion will be displayed in the cards. The basic objective behind the launch of the web portal is to create a single national database on soil health which can be used in the future for research and planning both by farmers and soil experts. The cards provide permanent identification and status of the land to farmers. This scheme has helped increase agricultural productivity and crop quality.

Agropedia

This is the social communications space for the AGROPEDIA users, which is constructed on web 3.0 technology. In contrast with the extension material, it provides different features like blog, forum, chat, wiki to share and learn agricultural information.

Agroforum: It is a platform where a registered user can post a question under any one of the forums and an expert on the related topic would reply and hence a conversation is opened.

Agrochat: It is an entirely new concept for an agricultural website where registered users can get involved in one to one as well as one to many chat. It is very simple and efficient to use too.

Agrowiki: It is developed by using the idea of 'Wiki', popularised by Wikipedia *i.e.* everyone is able to search and create content about agriculture, and share it with others. Here one can also visualize and upload images in addition to text. Agrowiki is related to agricultural domain, whereas Wikipedia is dealing with all types of information.

Agroblog: It is like a personal diary where all the registered users can share their experiences and other registered users can comment on them)

Challenges in Effective Use of e-Technology

In major India, ICT is a challenge as well as an opportunity. Illiteracy, poverty, poor financial conditions, lack of interest and hard work are the main constraints in the development of agriculture. Limited information is also a factor in restricting economic advancement for developing country like India. Especially agriculture sector is facing many problems to obtain new information about market price, weather updates and other related issues. In addition to the above, the following limitations are faced by the farming community.

☆ ICT infrastructure could develop by taking the advantage of existing infrastructures by which farmers can increase the acceptability of the new technology.

☆ It minimizes the costs of the technology and makes it affordable by the farmer communities.

☆ Inadequate infrastructure and appropriate ICT policies.

☆ High cost of available technologies.

☆ Lack of adequate resources like electricity, limited network coverage and low bandwidth, local languages *etc.* must be taken into account.

☆ The technology itself is not sufficient, but a well trained team is also required for the proper application of the technology.

☆ Lack of involvement of all stakeholders in planning, especially youth.)

☆ Inadequate collaboration and awareness of existing ICT facilities and resources.

☆ Inadequate and inappropriate credit facilities and systems.

☆ People (agents) who provide these ICT services to farmers also use the information for their own benefit.

☆ Developing countries have limited access to information sharing.

☆ The technology has not reached all the farmers.

☆ Most of the farmers are still ignorant about these technological developments and applications.

Chapter 10

e-Resources in Fisheries and Aquaculture

ICT's in Fisheries and Aquaculture

Electronic information resources play a vital role in the field of fisheries and aquaculture. The latest innovations of ICT's in fisheries sectors have brought about a tremendous change in the life styles of the fish farmers. Different initiatives in ICT's have been taken up which would also help in expanding and developing the fisheries technologies to the farmers. However, the rural people still have difficulties in accessing crucial information in forms they can understand in order to make timely decisions. New information and communication technologies are generating possibilities to solve problems of rural people and also to promote the agricultural production by providing scientific information to the farmers. But the rural communities still lack basic communication infrastructure.

New information and communication technologies (ICT's) are being used across the fisheries sector, from resource assessment, capture or culture to processing and commercialisation. Some are specialist applications such as sonar for locating fish. Others are general purpose applications such as Global Positioning Systems (GPS) used for navigation and location finding, mobile phones for trading, information exchange and emergencies, radio programming with fishing communities and web-based information and networking resources.

Introduction of mobile phones in India has brought about a tremendous change in fisheries sector. One result is a dramatic improvement in the efficiency and profitability of the fishing industry. As mobile phone service spread, it allowed fishermen to land their catches where there was profitable market. This reduced waste from between 5-8 per cent of total catch to close to zero and increased average profitability by around 8 per cent. At the same time, consumer prices fell by 4 per cent.

Different communication technologies have been used by the fishermen, entrepreneurs, aquaculturist, extension workers, *etc.* Of all these, radio has been found to be most widely used by farmers. Information on various innovations of fisheries technologies are being disseminated among the farmers. The internet is emerging as a tool with potential to contribute to rural development. Internet enables rural communities to receive information and assistance from other development organisations: offer opportunities for two-way and horizontal communication and for opening up communication channels for rural communities and development organisations.

It can facilitate dialogue among communities and with government planners, development agencies, researchers, and technical experts: encourage community participation in decision-making; coordinating local, regional and national development efforts for increased effectiveness; and help researchers, technicians, farmers and others in sharing information.

ICT Services in Fisheries and Aquaculture

Agricultural Technology Information Centre (ATIC)

It is not enough to generate information alone but it is also necessary to ensure that the required information is delivered to the end users at the earliest and with the least dissemination loss.

The establishment of agricultural technology information centres (ATIC) can forge a better interaction between researchers and technology users. It acts as a single window system with an objective to help farmers and other stakeholders to provide solutions to their agriculture related problems. This also helps in providing technological information along with technology inputs and products. Such information is useful for farmers, entrepreneurs, extension workers, NGOs and private sector organisations.

Kisan Call Centre (KCC)

The Department of Agriculture and Cooperation (DAC), Ministry of Agriculture and Farmers Welfare, Govt of India launched Kisan Call Centres across the country to deliver extension services to the farming community. A Kisan Call Centres consists of a complex of telecommunication infrastructure, computer support and human resources organized to respond the queries raised by farmers in their local languages.

Subject Matter Specialists (SMS) using telephone and computers, interact with farmers directly to understand the problems and answer the queries at the call centres. There are call centres in every state that are expected to handle traffic from any part of the country.

Helpline

The help lines address queries related at specific hours. The helpline number is advertised through mass media *viz.*, radio and press.

Aqua Service Centres

Many unemployed educated youths have started operating aqua service centres in the line of agri-clinics. These centres offer services like soil and water testing, feed analysis, seed quality testing (PCR test), disease diagnosis and market intelligence. They also sell inputs such as feed, fertilizers, pesticides, other therapeutics *etc.*

Aqua Choupal

Aqua choupal, the unique web based initiative of ITC Ltd. offers the farmers of the country all the information, products and services they need to enhance productivity, improve farm gate prize realization and cut transaction cost. Farmers can access information on weather, scientific farming practices and market prices through a web portal. Aqua choupal also facilitate the supply of high quality farm inputs as well as purchase of shrimps at their doorstep.

Rural Knowledge Centre

Rural Knowledge Centre is a part of a nationwide plan and has been set in motion in July 2004 by the Centre in collaboration with the states, NASSCOM, UNDP and a host of NGOs. Its primary aim is to set up multipurpose resource centres at the villages of the country. Each Knowledge Centre is run by local self help groups, and cater to knowledge based livelihoods and create income avenues for rural people, farming communities and disadvantaged people.

Cyber Extension

Internet enables rural communities to receive information and assistance from other development organisations: offer opportunities for two-way and horizontal communication and for opening up communication channels for rural communities and development organisations. It can facilitate dialogue among communities and with government planners, development agencies, researchers, and technical experts: encourage community participation in decision-making; coordinating local, regional and national development efforts for increased effectiveness; and help agricultural researchers, technicians, farmers and others in sharing information.

Sustainable Development through ICT in Fisheries and Aquaculture

The aquaculture and fisheries sector of developing countries are under tremendous pressure due to the increasing market orientation of aquaculture, the emergence of global markets and competition and increasing concern about food and environment. Diversification and intensification are some of the key factors for sustainable aquaculture development and therefore the regular information flow among farming communities, technical and marketing resources and other supplying institutions is a must for steady growth in the farm economy. Small holder farm families who comprise the majority of farming families are facing increased pressure to respond changing market demands.

The agricultural decisions and transactions in the developed world are now manipulated through digital networks. The internet and mobile telephones in particular, are used by governments to provide services to citizens (e-government).

e-governance can make governance more efficient and more effective by improving governmental process (e-administration), connecting citizens (e-citizens and e-services) and building external interactions (e-society). E-citizens, e-services and e-society are relatively new inclusions within the e-governance as they rely on the new Information and Communication technologies (ICT). Public extension systems require a paradigm shift from top-down, blanket dissemination of technological packages, towards providing producers with the knowledge and understanding.

Major Advantages of ICT Usage in the Fisheries

(i) Increasing Socio-economic Level of Fishermen

Usage of ICT tools such as GPS and sonar have been proved to increase the productivity and save the cost of the fishermen. GPS and sonar are able to mark the fishing spot and the fishermen can exactly go to the same location either at day or night. This ability is useful in term of saving the cost, time and energy of the fishermen. Not like the previous days, fishermen, with the existence of these tools, are able to come back with a bigger quantity of fish.

(ii) To increase ICT Knowledge and Skills

The easiness of learning process of the ICT tools such as GPS and sonar enable fishermen to learn it easily thus increasing their ICT knowledge and skills. On top of it, online services provided for fishermen such as fish online, e-declaration and e-fishermen have the ability to disseminate all the information needed by the fishermen. They can get all the information needed at any time and at any place: "Majority of the fishermen are not in a higher education group, but because of the learning process of these tools (GPS and sonar) is very easy, and they have no problem to learn it. It is true that they have low education background but it is not a problem for them *to learn how to use the GPS and sonar...*" "They can enhance their ICT knowledge with the assistance of the related agencies/associations for example they can check through online whether their smart card is still active or whether their fishing license is still active or not..." "Actually, they have no problems in learning the ICT, they enjoy using the services (online services) and facilities provided by the government..."

(iii) To Ease the Communication Process with Simple and Low Cost Communication

Wireless set and the mobile phone will help the fishermen to respond quickly to the market demand. Fishermen spend less time on idling on shore and at sea, whereas dealers go to the landing centers only when they receive the information (through wireless set and mobile phone) that the fishermen boats are about to dock. Besides, the wireless set and mobile phone can help the fishermen by providing the information of the related agencies on the places they can get a better price for their fish:

Enhancing the Safety Aspects of the Fisherman

ICT tools such as wireless set, mobile phone and GPS will enhance the safety aspects of the fishermen in the sea. Wireless set and mobile phone can be used to communicate with the colleagues and agencies officers if there is anything happening to them on the sea. GPS is helpful in assisting the fishermen to find their way back especially in a bad weather condition.

GPS, besides marking the fishing location for the fishermen, it is also responsible in informing the fishermen on any obstacles such as coral. Thus it can avoid any damage to the fishermen boat and more importantly it can avoid any accidents that might involve human life.

Useful Websites in the Field of Fishries

Following web sites will be useful to all the users who are interested to refer the information in the field in the fisheries.

Sl.No.	Organization/Institute	Website
1.	Zoological Survey of India (ZSI)	http://zsi.gov.in
2.	World Fishery Center	http://www. worldfisherycenter.org/
3.	World Aquaculture Society	http://www.was.org/
4.	National Institute of Oceanography	http://nio.org/
5.	Fishery Survey of India	http://fsi.gov.in
6.	Asian Fisheries Society	http://asianfisheriessociety.org
7.	Bay of Bengal Programme (BOB)	http://www.bobpigo.org
8.	Rajiv Gandhi Centre for Aquaculture (RGCA)	rgcaho@gmail.com
9.	Network of Aquaculture Centers in Asia-Pacific (NACA)	http://www.enaca.org/
10.	National Marine Fisheries Service (NMFS)	http://www.nmfs.noaa.gov/
11.	National Centre for Sustainable Coastal Management (NCSCM)	http://www.ncscm.org
12.	National Centre for Cold Chain Development (NCCD)	http://nhb.gov.in

Leading Fishing Websites of the World

http://www.bassproshops.com

Bass Pro Shops is America's leading outdoor retailer with stores across America and Canada. Every Bass Pro Shops store still offers an incredible array of fishing and boating equipment. They are also the premier shopping destination for hunting, camping, and outdoor cooking gear as well as outdoor footwear and nature-themed gifts. You will have a difficult time not finding what you're looking for on their website.

http://www.bestbassfishinglures.com

This site is all about bass fishing lures made for catching largemouth bass and smallmouth bass. Very informative site that covers all the better bass fishing lures that every angler should carry from jigs to jitterbugs.

http://www.theessentialfly.com

Award winning website and great customer service. A great resource for fly fishing information and videos. They cover and sell a large range of fishing flies and fly materials for trout, salmon, bass, grayling and other species, all delivered world-wide.

http://www.basslures.net

The Bass Lures Blog is a bass fishing website with information for the beginner or professional. You will find informational articles on lures, product reviews, how-to's and guest posts from anglers from all over.

http://www.fishfinders.info

Provides unbiased user reviews of the latest fish finder models. Also, lists price comparisons and spec comparisons. Make sure to visit this site before you purchase your next fish finder.

http://www.theoutdoorsmensvoice.com

The Outdoorsmen's Voice is a community of members who love to hunt and fish. There are multiple forums on the site that cover all different aspects of the outdoors. Visit today and join a discussion on a variety of fishing topics.

http://www.fishfinderreviews.net

There are so many fish finders on the market that it can be very time consuming finding the right one. This site reduces that time spent searching and helps you find the right fish finder for your boat and style of fishing. Fish finders are expensive, so it's important to do your research before buying. Take some time to read the reviews and comparison charts on this site before making a purchase.

Chapter 11

Management of Agricultural Information and Knowledge

An Overview

Agricultural development in developing countries face constrained such as, access to appropriate technologies, immense institutional weaknesses and deep problems with the organization and management of research, education, and extension systems. Many countries and agricultural systems thus remain mired in underdevelopment and face major barriers to the use of knowledge and innovation for development. However, there are many governments who took active steps in organizational, technological, institutional, and policy innovations that are transforming agriculture and leading to growth and development. The World Development Report 2008 emphasizes the importance of knowledge in bringing about innovation. The report refers to a series of mutually supportive, often knowledge-intensive, innovations that enable a country's agricultural producers to move up the value chain in international agricultural export markets. The strategy is to bring about new or adapted knowledge to produce innovations that increase agricultural productivity and reduce poverty.

The World Bank in its World Development Report 1998 which is dealt with only the theme 'Knowledge for Development' has very skeptical in delineating the role of knowledge in the issues like knowledge supporting lifelong learning, helping the poor earn more income, getting useful information to the poor, improving governance. In addition to this, it has advocated that for developing countries, the new information and communication technologies hold enormous potential. People in remote communities the world over can have access to knowledge beyond the dreams of anyone in the industrialized countries even a quarter century ago. It is evident that information and knowledge has the greatest potential for development, if managed to communicate in right time to the right user in right manner.

Encumbrance of Information in Sustainable Agriculture

Today verybody will be of unanimous opinion that the exchange of information and knowledge by individuals and communities using new information and communications technologies (ICTs) certainly affects in achieving sustainable development and food security in the 21st century. There are several instances in which the ability of governments to predict areas of food insecurity and vulnerability using appropriate information and software tools, so that action can be taken to prevent or reduce the likelihood of an emergency. The bright example is the proper prediction on severe cyclonic storm 'Falaine' on October 2013 by the Indian Meteorological Department and right dissemination of information which did save the lives of at least 9000 people. Use of right information at the right time in right manner can save lives and improve livelihoods. Information can only empower when the user has access to it. Leaving aside mass media such as radio and television, information used to be disseminated in paper-based form, and it had to be brought physically to the user. More recently digital media such as diskettes and CD-ROMs, online, Internet, social networking etc, are frequently used for particular dissemination functions. These early digital technologies quickly led to the emergence of wide-area connectivity through the Internet, overcoming the limitations of paper-based dissemination programmes. The exploitation of the technology revolution has made information on agriculture available world-wide and on-demand. In the context of FAO, approximately 1,000 users per year requested information from the FAOSTAT database in the 1980s when it was held on a mainframe computer, whereas the Internet version available through WAICENT currently has more than 60,000 user sessions per month (FAO).

Global Agricultural Information

Generally developed countries and some international organizations generate large scale agricultural information with a purpose of universal and global access to information for sustainable, equitable development. Leading partners of agricultural research organizations are to create opportunities for the development and dissemination of information and knowledge from a variety of sources, in a variety of languages. In addition, the aim should be to support indigenous capacity and create the conditions for more effective generation and dissemination of content Some leading agricultural organizations including FAO continuously provide support in the use of specialized tools and applications for information delivery and communication in the areas of agricultural and allied sectors development.

Most of the issues to be addressed in agriculture require information from many disciplines, making it necessary to access many types of information resources. More recent developments in information management at the global level have enabled the establishment of distributed networks of databases, online resources, digital contents in library systems, consortia, development of institutional repositories, open access which lend themselves to the requirements stated above and improving the access to the wealth of information available. The new technologies can also improve the effectiveness of searching and retrieving relevant data and information across distributed networks. Some leading commercial database producers and leading national and international agricultural institutes and organisations have taken up new approaches to accessing information that could have major implications internationally.

A web-based information/knowledge management system is being developed with the aim of creating a specialized gateway. The system will provide a framework with a comprehensive set of web-based modular functions geared to aiding the administration, organization, indexing, cross-referencing, uploading and retrieval of information in a decentralized and participatory world-wide network.

Digital Contents in Agriculture: Creation and Management

Libraries used to create contents in different manner and most information services are contents created from the library collection and repackaged to tailor the needs of the users. The contents created must serve the users community so that they can derive utmost satisfaction with such contents. Digitization is basically done for the documents which are of research use and needs archival preservation. In order to manage the digitization process effectively the information manager has to assure the basic essential requirements such as, digital content component requirements; development of institutional repositories; network access to evaluated content resources from non-commercial web sources; network access to commercially published agricultural content literature in digital form; digital reformatting of printed content; digital data content capture, preservation, curatorial and preservation services for visualization and presentation of data resources related to agriculture; and the development of cyber infrastructure and grid computing environments required for networked agricultural scientific data resources. The institutions desiring to preserve their research outputs are to develop institutional repositories for which digital library is the only answer.

Some libraries have fragile documents which are required to be preserved for the future. Such types of documents are old manuscripts, old music recordings, newspapers, cultural artifacts, etc need preservation. Other important documents are local history collections of a library which are decaying day by day need to be preserved through electronically. Most university and public libraries have very old books, annual reports, research reports convocation speeches which are also very useful publications in specific subjects which do not come under copyright restrictions may be digitized. Other types of documents which need digitization are endangered/threatened species of plants and animals, collection for disabled and children. Content creation of all those materials may be taken up by the libraries so that the digitization effort will be a successful.

Agricultural Knowledge Network

The formation of communication network in agriculture is an essential task for the authority to ensure transmission of information from one end to other. National Agricultural Library of US has developed Agricultural Network Information Center

Alliance (AgNIC) which involves multiple institutions working in partnership to facilitate access to quality information resources related to all aspects of agricultural, food, and natural resources. AgNIC institutions provide a growing array of services to multiple audiences. AgNIC provides rapid network access to a broad range of evaluated agriculture-related information and educational resources by employing the most current information networking technologies. All member partners of the network are to contribute their digitized resources and metadata and vocabulary standards, and have recently implemented portal and web services applications serving the national agricultural community. The following activities would improve the functioning of the network:

☆ Digital reformatting and preservation of printed agricultural documents and publications as well as related grey literature resources in agricultural-related disciplines;

☆ Digital capture and preservation of web content resources (commercial and non-commercial) related to the agricultural sciences;

☆ The development of distributed network technology infrastructure required to maintain and preserve agricultural research data;

☆ The development of data tools for manipulation, analysis, and presentation of networked content and resources.

Agricultural Libraries and Information Centres

Library's pre-eminence role in developing the information and knowledge dissemination in support of scientists, researchers, students, and the general public, in order to enhance the development of agriculture is highly acknowledged. All the agricultural university libraries and ICAR institutes' libraries in India should collaborate in developing a knowledge management strategy.

In fulfillment of the developing the proper knowledge management system, the library selects, acquires, manages, delivers, and preserves a diversified and broad range of information resources related to agricultural topics. The library delivers programs that support teaching and learning, fosters information competence, and provides expertise, tools, and services facilitating access to and management of the nation's information assets. Every agricultural library promotes the dissemination of right information as their chief resource and service for agricultural information.

Library's management and staff should develop the vision of library role in management of agricultural information and knowledge. The National Agricultural Library of every country should take the lead in developing agricultural information gateway serving the agricultural requirement of the national as well as the people of the country. The National Agricultural Library endeavors to be the premier source of agricultural information, serving the public and the all agricultural stake holders to meet the challenges of the 21st century. The National Agricultural Library-the ultimate source for agricultural information, current and historical, dedicated to providing the right information products for the world of agriculture.

The National Agricultural Library of a country is the centerpiece of a dynamic national agricultural information network providing essential and cost-effective access to and digital dissemination/delivery of comprehensive content media and related services in agricultural sciences and allied disciplines, in support of scientific research, education, industry, and the general public. The National Agricultural Library serves as the country's hub for improving the quality of life

Recenty Changing Trends of Agricultural Information Scenario

The changing trend of information has profound impact on information intensive activities, including the agricultural sciences and related disciplines. In the library and information services area, as well as in the conduct of agricultural research, these dynamic forces of change have the potential to transform the way information is created, accessed, and used. Changes are affecting the way science is conducted and the way new knowledge created. Fundamental changes are having a significant impact on agricultural information and library-related activities, moving toward transformational changes that present both opportunities and threats.

Major Trends in the Conduct of Scientific Research

Multidisciplinary nature of agricultural science domain involving traditional science fields as well as social science specialties (*e.g.*, Food and Nutrition, renewable energy sources, and environmental remediation); Increasing inter-disciplinary and multi-disciplinary team based research in agricultural science-related discipline. Research performed by teams composed of scientists with differing specialties working at multiple locations. These trends are especially evident in: Increasing use of instrumentation which generates massive sets of data; Vastly increased amounts of data requiring data management tools especially in fields involving GIS and genomic data; Mixed state/Federal/commercial inter-sector partnerships; Increased need for consultative services, taxonomic expertise, research tool development and creation, and archival preservation yielding a hierarchy of core competencies; Increasing functionality of network resources, tools, and capabilities; Shifts from basic/fundamental to applied and methods research; Acceleration of cycles of discovery; Focus on capturing processes, not just end results; More open forms of publications and artifact sharing; More continuous (vs. batch) and open forms of scholarly communication; Enhanced sharing, re-use and multi-use of resources; New levels of comprehensive access to archival and real-time multimedia data, information and knowledge.

Major Trends in Information Services

Increasing need to balance access, preservation, and the integration of information content with data resources; Increasing demand for services that are available anywhere and anytime; Distributed, integrated, and mobile network services; Services that are cross-walked, that balance virtual and physical and that are connected and distributed.

Proliferation of information resource content - published and unpublished - formal and informal; Mixed printed and digital content resources; Multiple audience segments: scientific, educational, administrative, policy makers, public; Increased demand for libraries to translate and leverage research results, data expression into usable venues and Increased demand for access to Grey literature of agricultural sciences.

Web has Vast Reservoir of Information Resources: As per one estimate there are 15 million web sites and 10 billion web pages. In order improve the web-based services there is a greater necessity to access links to evaluated digital content resources from non-commercial research sources. It is imperative on the part of the information centers to undertake proper evaluation, selection, capture, integration, and preservation of relevant web content for establishing and maintaining links through a customizable interface. Access is provided through cross database federated search engines and discovery tools. Such a decentralized model for global access is the basis for the developing web portals in specific subjects in agriculture. The use of thesaurus tools and controlled vocabulary in conjunction with web content linking ensure logical and relevant search results for linked access to non-commercial web content.

Digital Preservation Formatting for Print Content

Digital preservation formatting for print content is another component of agricultural knowledge management concept. Development of structures for capturing, preserving of digitally reformatted printed content requires standards development and implementation through a nationally coordinated program by which digital scanning, preservation reformatting, and metadata standards are developed.

In the agricultural sciences especially, grey literature capture and reformatting is a critical area for concentration. ICAR has developed eGranth project in which the print documents are reformatted and properly scanned and digitized which are browsable in a networked environment and for longer digital preservation of the intellectual contents.

Cyber Infrastructure Development in Agricultural Science

Increasingly, agricultural scientific research activities posit the need for development of a cyber-infrastructure consisting of high-performance computational resources, massive data storage repositories, next-generation networks, digital library databases, application frameworks, and e-research/e-science tools. Such a shared cyber-infrastructure is needed to support scientists and researchers engaged in team-based research.

Developments in digital and network technologies offer opportunities for agricultural stakeholders in India to collaboratively develop library's cyber-infrastructure services for agricultural scientific researchers employing high-speed broadband digital networks, data acquisition, repository and curatorial services, as well as tools to facilitate data exploration, analysis, visualization, and discovery. Such a pragmatic cyber-infrastructure development effort supports global science in general and agriculture in particular. These emerging research in agricultural fields require high-capacity mass storage systems, large-scale data repositories, and cyber-infrastructure networking technologies.

Each library must plan to develop these research data services complement to information management and delivery services for its own library staff and other scientists in providing integrated access to scientific articles and research publication literature content. The development of one library's agricultural cyber-infrastructure results from recent advances in agriculture and the life sciences that require large-scale distributed repositories, as well as grid computing functionality. Such an agricultural cyber-infrastructure is needed to address the need for distributed access to a growing body of scientific data, as well as the development of tools for analysis, manipulation, preservation, and repurposing of large scale data sets. Essentially, enhanced data and system applications, capabilities, and efficiencies are required to create team-based digital science using community gateways.

Developing a Global Digital Library for Agriculture

A new age has dawned in scientific and engineering research, pushed by continuing progress in computing, information, and communication technology, and pulled by the expanding complexity, scope, and scale of today's challenges. The capacity of this technology has crossed thresholds that now make possible a comprehensive cyber-infrastructure on which to build new types of scientific and engineering knowledge environments and organizations and to pursue research in new ways and with increased efficacy." Global cyber-infrastructure in support of agricultural science and research can provide a platform for routine, effective distance-independent activities of knowledge communities. Such virtual communities are needed to address the increasingly global challenges presented by emerging diseases, food safety, and environmental degradation. In the future, world-scale collaborative teams will depend upon a global cyber-infrastructure capable of offering new options for what is done, how it is done, and who participates.

The global library community now has the opportunity and responsibility to move from concept to implementation.

Developing a Global Digital Library for Agriculture is an essential component for creation of a trusted environment for knowledge access and creation. This GDLA will support more extensive collaborations that will reduce research disparities, enhance research productivity, and address global challenges. The GDLA as a global information infrastructure is needed to assure advancement of the agricultural sciences for the future. It is essential to foster the pursuit of knowledge by providing a space for intellectual exchange, research, learning and discovery.

The real dissemination of information is achieved, if the material communicated to the users is perceived to be used. The stage has already come for developing digital libraries so that the communication of information is easy and accessible to the users. Agriculture is the most vibrant subject area where information and knowledge management appears to be imminent. Right communication of information in right time in right manner to the right stakeholders of agriculture will certainly improve the whole farming system in the world. In this direction the role of libraries appears to be very significant. Because, information is acquired by the libraries, processed and disseminated to the user groups. Managing a good communication strategy helps develop a good information system. The emerging information and communication technologies and mobile phone improves the information dissemination system. The Internet has done gargantuan task in building a virtual world where information is made available in a network system. The digital library system has revitalized the information retrieval system enabling instant access to knowledge.

Chapter 12

Application of Social Networking Services for Library

Introduction : An Overview

In foreign countries use of social network in academic libraries and even in public libraries are found more as compared to Indian academic libraries and not in public libraries. Social media are computer-mediated tools that allow people or companies to create, share, or exchange information, career interests, ideas, and pictures/videos in virtual communities and networks. Social media is used by libraries to deliver a blend of customer service, news and updates, content/collection promotion, dissemination of the institutions' research output, provision of educational tools and resources and for building relationships both within and outside of the institution. A wide range of social media channels are used, but as yet there is limited differentiation between how they are used. Recently there seems to have been a shift from using social media as the voice of the institution to being the voice of a librarian within the institution. This 'humanization' of libraries using social media is seen by some as key to utilising social media effectively (Gauntner Witte 2014). Social media has the potential to facilitate much closer relationships between libraries and their patrons. Current usage of social media by the library community generally remains ad hoc and somewhat experimental, but the uptake of these tools is accelerating, and they will likely play an increasingly important role in library service provision and outreach in the future.

Social Networking Approach

The term "Social Networking" refers to a range of web-enabled/it-enabled software programs that allow users to interact and work collaboratively with other users. It includes ability to browse, search, invite friends to connect and interact, share film reviews, comments, blog entries, favorites, discussions, events, videos, ratings, music, classified ads, tag and classified information and more.

A social network allows individual to join and create a personal profile, then formally connect with other users of the systems as social friend. It can be expressed as social connecting sites among the social user in web 2.0 domain. The potential of social networks to be relevant to information seeking and sharing from the more specialist web 2.0 sites. Social network sites as web-based services that allow individuals to (1) construct a public or semi-public profile within a bounded system, (2) articulate a list of other users with whom they share a connection, and (3) view and traverse their list of connections and those made by others within the system. The newly proposed Deleting Online Predators Act of 2006 states the term "commercial social networking website" means a commercially operated Internet Web site that allowsusers to create web pages or profiles that provide information about themselves and are available to others users; and offers a mechanism for communication with other users, such as a forum, chat room, email, or instant messenger. Social network analysis views social relationships in terms of nodes and ties. Nodes are the individual actors within the networks, and ties are the relationships between the actors. There can be many kinds of ties between the nodes. In its simplest form, a social network is a map of all of the relevant ties between the nodes being studied. The network can also be used to determine the social capital of individual actors.

Potential of Social Networking

Social networking can be relevant to information seeking and sharing on information retrieval perspective by providing speed and quick information to the information community by connecting and collecting digital information required by the user. Social networking sites like MySpace, FaceBoook represent a new and powerful service through web 2.0. User can connect to other user from various part of internet domain by applying social networking tools for information communication, organization and information distribution. The idea behind the social networks is that they operate on many levels, right from the family level up to the level of the nations. They have come to play a very important role in determining how problems are solved, how organizations are run, and the efficiency with which individuals succeed in achieving their goals. Social networking websites function like an online community of internet users. Depending on the website in question, many of these online community members share a common interest such as hobbies, religion, or politics. Once you are granted access to a social networking website you can begin to socialize. This socialization may include reading the profile pages of other members and possibly even contacting them. Some solid motives behind social network are:

☆ Anticipated Reciprocity - contribute valuable information; expect that one will receive useful help and information in return

☆ Increased Recognition - individuals want recognition for their contributions

☆ Sense of efficacy – contributors believe that they have had some effect on this environment or community

☆ User Participation- User wants more participation and contribution in social web. More social and collaboration. Social networking could enable librarians and patrons not only to interact, but to share and change resources dynamically in an electronic medium

☆ Embrace radical trust

☆ Engage in rapid change-drastic and rapid change has been seen since past decade

☆ Communally innovative- It rests on the foundation of libraries as a community service, but understands that as communities change, libraries must not only change with them, they must allow users to change the library

☆ Open access movement- Libraries make collections available via open, personalized, interactive services that encourage content creation, editing, commenting, bookmarking, rating, tagging, *etc.* by users

☆ Multimedia enabled

Features of Social Networking Services

Social networking in the field of information landscape can be great contributor to the field of information poor society. It has several unique features that can serve the user community where availability of resource is a great challenge to library field. Library should experiment and come forward to accept this new budding technology. It has some major features like social collaboration, easy surfing, more participation, private messaging can be easily possible by communicating thousands networks, discussion forums, events management, blogging and commenting, media uploading, multimedia enabled, interactive and collaborative learning are some of the important features that you can see in social networking.

Web Technology Services and Libraries

The major Web 2.0 services cover a wide variety of manners in which users or patrons can collaborate and communicate and are dynamic in that they allow for users to interact with other user created information. One of those services is a blog, which "is a web page that consists predominantly of user-supplied content" (Boxen, 2008). This could take the form of a journal entry, or could contain news, links, or downloads.

Library collections now include a mix of traditional materials (printed books, serials, audio-visual) and emerging formats (e-books, e-serials, e-newspapers, e-theses and dissertations, Internet resources, digital objects).

Library 3.0 and the technological changes that will follow it will be a vital and exciting part of how libraries develop and extend their formal and informal learning programs. Social media allow us to improve our online resources, which will ensure that our services remain relevant to the communities we serve, and improve access to informal self-education and lifelong learning opportunities.

Practicing Social Networking in Library Services

Social Networks or social software can be used for providing user centric service in social library environment. User attitude towards library is changing day by day. User wants most practical and speed information in e-learning age. But providing quick and easy retrieval information to user is a great challenge to library. Therefore library should find and search some new techniques for impacting valuable information to the user. Virtual Reference Desk (VRD) can be performed by wikipedia.You can planed, design and disseminate information to patrons by KM Wiki. Marketing of library services can be possible by using social software tools like Podcast, YouTube, Blogger, SecondLife, Ning *etc.* Catalogue some of your library books on library thing. Library can host their personal websites in PBwiki or blogger. Library version can be possible by secondlife. Start a library podcast and interview students, teachers, patrons and members of the community. Digital video library can be framed by using the most successful tool like YouTube in Library. Impacting and planning online course curriculum in online learning environment by PBWiki. Support just-in-time reference, since students may find it easier and more comfortable to communicate with a librarian through this medium than in traditional ways. Take online assistance by implementing chat reference *i.e.* IM in library. Library assignment and teaching scheduled through social software tools like Jhoomla.Professionanls can put their collections on flicker. Footnote.com may be used to learn about history of library. After all it will be helpful to provide the means to learn more about students, which can help libraries, better meet their needs.

Chapter 13

Use of Internet Based e-Resources and Web Services

Introduction

The Internet is a worldwide system of interconnected computer networks. The computers and computer networks exchange information using TCP/IP (Transmission Control Protocol/Internet Protocol) to communicate with each other. The computers are connected via the telecommunications networks, and the Internet can be used for e-mailing, transferring files and accessing information on the World Wide Web.

The World Wide Web is a system of Internet servers that use HTTP (Hypertext Transfer Protocol) to transfer documents formatted in HTML (Hypertext Mark-up Language). These are viewed by using software for web browsers such as Netscape, Safari, Google Chrome and Internet Explorer. Hypertext enables a document to be connected to other documents on the web through hyperlinks. It is possible to move from one document to another by using hyperlinked text found within web pages.

Nowadays, there are several ways that enable us to access the Internet. Technology is keep improving, method to access the Internet also increase. People can now access Internet services by using their cell phone, laptop and various gadgets. The numbers of Internet service providers are also keep increasing. For example in Malaysia, there are many Internet service providers such as TM Net, Maxis, Digi, Celcom, Umobile, *etc.*

Communication is becoming much easier than before due to the appearance of Internet. One of the conveniences is that messages, in the forms of email, can be sent at any corner of the world within fractions of seconds. Besides that, email also facilitated mass communication which means that one sender reaches many receivers. Some of the services made available due to Internet include video conferencing, live telecast, music, news, e-commerce, *etc.*

Internet History

The rapid development of Internet started at the early 1960, paralleled with the developments of the computers. Those scientists and researcher started to realize a great vision, a future that everyone will be able to communicate by using their computers. J.C.R. Licklider of MIT, first proposed a global network of computers in 1962 and followed by Leonard Kleinrock from MIT, who published the first paper on packet switching theory.

ARPANET, which is the former of Internet, was a project launched by Military Department of USA. It was brought online at Oct 29, 1969 by Charley Kline at UCLA, when he attempted to perform a remote login from UCLA to SRI. In order to get attentions from public, they made the first public demonstration of ARPANET at an international conference at October 1972.

The initial ARPANET was a single,closed network. In order to communicate with an ARPANET, one had to be attached to another ARPANET IMP (interface message processor). Hence, the disadvantages of single network were realized and lead the development of open-architecture network and also different protocols of internetworking, which enable multiple networks can be joined together. E-mail was adapted for ARPANET by Ray Tomlinson of BBN in 1972. The telnet protocol, enabling logging on to a remote computer, was published as a Request for Comments (RFC) in 1972. RFC's are a means of sharing developmental work throughout community. The FTP protocol, enabling file transfers between Internet sites, was published as an RFC in 1973, and from then on RFC's were available electronically to anyone who had use of the FTP protocol.

Before the TCP/IP protocol was introduced by BoB Kahn, the networking protocols used for the ARPANET was NCP, Network Control Protocols. NCP did not have the ability to address networks further downstream than a destination IMP on ARPANET. By 1980, the Internet had reached a certain level of maturity and started to exposed to public usage more and more often. At the same time, French launched the Minitel project to bring data networking into everyone's home by gave away a free terminal to each household requested.

At the 1990s, the Internet predecessor, ARPANET finally came to an end, and replaced by the NSFNET which serve as a backbone connecting regional networks in USA. However, the most significant changes of Internet at 1990s was the World Wide Web(WWW) application which truly brought Internet to our daily life. Various technologies such as VoIP, HTML, web browsers with graphical user interfaces, P2P file sharing, instant messaging which is very familiar to us nowadays.

Internet Usage and Benefit

It is globalization and modernization nowadays, Internet become more and more useful and come into everyday life. From the early days of computers to now, communication between people to people has been the technology's most frequent used. People using the Internet to sent or received email. Using email leads people to spend more time online, encourages their use of the Internet for information, entertainment. All this can save time and money because it is consider efficiency enough and always is cheaper. As new Internet communication services arise such as those instant messaging, chat rooms, online games, auctions (eBay), and my groups, they become instantly popular.[9]

Information searching is the second basic Internet function. Many use the Internet to search and download some of the free, useful computer software that provided by the developers on computers worldwide. The only major problem would be finding what you need among the storehouses of data found in databases and libraries. It is therefore necessary to explain the two major methods of accessing computers and locating files without the information retrieval function would not be possible. There are also educational resources on the Internet. They are in various forms such as journals and databases on different types of knowledge. For example, people can access online journals, or learning languages. There are also special homepages on special topics or subjects of interest. These sites are very helpful to those who are doing academic research or even teachers. This will go a long way to improve their knowledge to make them more competitive and knowledgeable. There are now even virtual libraries and full degree programs, all available online.

In fact, it is undeniable a trend of commerce on the Internet. The communication facilities have now rapidly become integrated as core business tools such as Internet market, banking, advertisement and so on. Thus most of the business functions are communicative in nature. Users or consumer need not to waste their time on queue up waiting their transaction and service. Internet makes communication with customers and other business partner even to some respondent if related to some online survey.

Internet Application

Network applications are among the most important parts in computer network – if we couldn't get any useful applications, there would be no use designing networking protocols to support them. Over half a century ago, a variety of intelligent network applications were created. These applications included the classic text-based applications that become popular in the 1970s and later developed into e-mail, remote access to computers, file transfers, newsgroup and text chat in 1980s. As time went by they introduced more killer applications like the World Wide Web, encompassing Web surfing, search and electronic commerce in middle 1990s. Applications like instant messaging with buddy list and P2P file sharing were introduced at the end of millennium.

Nowadays, instead of the already applications was updated, they also include successful audio and video applications including Internet telephony, video sharing and streaming, social networking applications, Internet radio and IP television (IPTV). In addition, the increased penetration of residential broadband access and ubiquity increased access wireless applications set the stage for an exciting future. At the core of the network applications development writing programs that take place on different end systems communicated with each other through the network.

For example, the Web application, there are two different programs that communicate with each other: the browser program running on the user's host desktop, laptop. PDA, cell phone and so on; and the Web server program running in the Web server host. As another example, in a P2P file sharing systems have a program in each host community to participate in file sharing. In this case, the programs on the various hosts may be similar or identical. This basic design – namely, confining application software to the end.

Base Concept of Internet

Internet is a brand-new world with its own language. It is a computer network of networks. It is a vast information superhighway that facilitates communication between computer users both nationally and internationally. It enables computers of all kinds to share services and communicate directly as if they are part of a giant global computing machine.

With the arrival of Information Technology especially Internet technology in a significant way in India, Information, services and products are undergoing rapid changes in all sectors including the services being provided by the various government agencies to citizens.

India has been connected to the Internet since 1989. Currently, it is estimated that there are about 100 million Internet users in this country. Access to the Internet is provided by four government organizations - Education and Research Network (ERNET), which provides service to the academic and research segments of society, National Informatics Centre (NIC) which serves government agencies, Software Technology Parks of India (STPI) which acts as a developer for software development companies, and Videsh Sanchar Nigam Limited (VSNL), which is the government's international telecommunications service provider. VSNL also provides the only Internet Connection available for the general public called Gateway Internet Access Service (GIAS) and MTNL, Mumbai. Because the government owns/operates the entire ISP (Internet Service Provider) in India, government policy is the main constraint on Internet development. The Internet flourishes in an open competitive environment. The dominance/interference of a government in this industry is a negative factor.

Popular Web Browsers for Internet

Logo	Web Browser
	Internet Explorer
	Firefox (also called Mozilla Firefox)

Logo	Web Browser
	Chrome
	Safari
	Opera
	Netscape Navigator
	Camino
	SeaMonkey
	K-Meleon
	Galeon
	Konqueror
	Maxthon Browser

Logo	Web Browser
	Flock (web browser)
	Midori
	Uzbl
	RockMelt
	Voyager
	Dillo Web Browser
	Slim Browser
	KidRocket
	Epic

World Wide Web

WWW (World Wide Web) is an Internet standard for distributed hypertext, in which the documents can have links to other documents that can be anywhere on the Internet. For example, if a document mentions "Constitution," clicking on that word might bring up a copy of the Constitution. Clicking on the Second Amendment might bring up a discussion of that topic, which might include links to articles at a completely different site, and so on. WWW is a revolutionary technology. Programs for browsing World Wide Web such as CELLO and Mosaic are available for most platforms, including Windows, Mac, X-Windows, and many more. Mosaic and CELLO are very nice GUI (Graphical User Interface) programs, which allow you to point and click to navigate most of the common Internet. It needs an IP (Internet Protocol) network connection to use WWW directly from the machine. However, one can also use a character-based program called "lynx" from your UNIX shell account to view WWW resources. With lynx, no images are displayed, but most of the info gets across. (Images are nice, but can also slow down WWW access a lot). With lynx, the IP connection is your service provider's which is likely much faster connection than your IP connection at home.

For a graphical WWW interface on your Windows machine, various Windows TCP/IP packages exist, including solid shareware ones like Trumpet, and good supported commercial packages from NetManage, Frontier and others. Most IP packages support serial protocols for connecting directly to the Internet over a modem.

e-Mail Service

In most academic and research institutions, e-mail has already become a replacement or alternative to internal memoranda. The ability to easily set up and maintain Internet mailing lists can be applied in the intranet context to support group communication. Mailing list can be archived and the archive made available from the intranet's web server to allow a group memory to be developed. Mailing list archives are also more accurate than traditional meeting minutes and means that groups no longer need to dedicate someone to make notes of their decisions.

Effective communication has been the need of the hour to bridge the time gap, which has enabled to communicate between the users around the world. E-mail refers to transmission of information from one person to another person electronically to foster time saving device. It is this technology that has minimized the popularity of postal services in the country for communication. Through this technology, the information in MBPS containing text, images, video, audio can be sent as an attachment in a very short time to the destination.

Library has been extending the e-mail service to the users and it has been widely used by the library professionals for carrying out library inhouse activities and services especially for ordering, enquiring or canceling order for documents and communication with peer groups; obtaining for reprints etc and are moving towards paperless society as far as communication is concerned.

File Transfer Protocol (FTP)

It is the Internet file transfer protocol/program used to transfer files. Using FTP to get files to the Internet-connected machine from other Internet machines. FTP sites listed here support anonymous logins, meaning anyone can use them by giving "anonymous" for Name and e-mail address as Password.

Telnet

Telnet is a facility through which logging into a remote site is much like logging directly there. Telnet sites are reference either by site name or numeric IP address. This application allows the user to login into the remote host, run software and read data files residing on the remote host. In most of the implementations of Telnet, a valid login and password is required.

Discussion Forums

A discussion list is a listing of e-mail names and addresses that are grouped under a single name. Through e-mail, everyone in the discussion group gets a copy of the message. These are frequently found on intranets, where they offer a kind of collaborative work area. Ideas can be exchanged on a variety of topics. Discussion groups are often managed using a list server operated using the same software that runs many Internet mailing lists. A number of freely available software packages are widely used, notably LISTSERV *etc.*

Newsgroups

Usenet newsgroups are like conferences or forums on a Bulletin Board System. Generally, anyone can read and post messages to a newsgroup. There are elaborate newsgroup hierarchies, starting with sci, talk, comp, alt, rec, and so on. Newsgroup postings expire after a certain amount of time regardless of whether read them or not.

Virtual Reference Service

Library services are being delivered to the remote users. New techniques in delivering information in various formats including electronic documents as alternatives to paper based documents. These methods of delivery include e-mail messages, FTP, putting information on bulletin boards or home pages on the Internet. This will avoid errors of transcriptions, reduce time and cost involved provides flexibility of timings and overcome barriers of distance.

Virtual Reference Service provides professional reference service to users anywhere anytime, through an international, digital network of libraries. This service is a real-time reference service via the Internet by making use of valuable resources. These advantages are possible because of digital uniqueness of documents and technology. The unique nature of digital reference introduces a new realm of issues and challenges. The need for guidelines and standards becomes even more important as consortium-wide digital reference services continue to evolve. Further, the improved facility of distribution and scanning make it possible to extend benefits to materials that are in non- digital format. The web, as a research tool allows the librarians to produce and deliver the information in electronic format, thus enhancing the level and access to a larger audience.

Online Public Access Catalogue

The library is a service-oriented institution which facilitates the users with its rich information resources through catalogue. With the advancement of Information and Communication technology, applications of Computer technology with dedicated library software's has enabled the libraries to develop new service known as Online Public Access Catalogue (OPAC) to the users. This reflects the library holdings in machine-readable format providing various searching access points like author, title, call number, Keywords *etc.*

The development of information technology and library software's in different platforms has enabled the library and information centers to host their bibliographical records on the Internet termed as Web OPAC. The OPAC in the networked environment is confined to the users within a campus, whereas the Web-OPAC extends its identity to the world by putting its resources made available in the bibliographical format. The Internet supports a variety of on-line services, and a number of tools are available to enable people to make good use of these, including: telnet, FTP, Gopher, Veronica, Archie, Wide Area Information Servers (WAIS), and the World-Wide Web (WWW). Now the library holdings are not only confined to library premises, but it can be hosted on the Internet revealing the collections of the library to the world. This facilitates the users to search the availability of documents in the library irrespective of location either by author, title, subject *etc.*

Document Delivery Service

Document Delivery is a term used in libraries to refer to the process of acquiring a copy of an item, which the home library does not own and does not intend to buy in the original. Thus, it could mean Inter-library Loan, the process whereby copies of books are borrowed from resourceful library to other libraries or copies of articles are obtained from them. As electronic journals become widely available, the boundaries between secondary abstracting and indexing services and the primary journals are obscured. Under Document Delivery Service, a print copy of the article/document can be delivered to the user using preferably Information Technology gadgets. The best example today are JCCC@UGC Infonet, JCCC@INDEST and JCCC@CeRa.

Content Alert Service

Contents alert services are available for free on the Internet. For instance, Elsevier's Science Direct is an example of a service offered by a major publisher that includes alerting services for their journals. The options include a search alert that lets you input author names, subject words, *etc.*; a volume/issue alert to discover when a new issue appears; and a citation alert that notifies you when an indicated article has been cited by someone in a newer article.

The American Chemical Society (ACS) Publications Division offers a similar service for its 30+ journals, ASAP Alerts and Table of Contents Alerts. ASAP stands for "As Soon As Publishable," so when one of the articles enters the database, you are notified immediately via e-mail that includes a link to the article. The American Chemical Society - Table of Contents Alerts is also an e-mail notification service, but it comes out only when the entire contents of a new issue are posted on the Web.

Access to Full Text e-journals/Databases

Electronic media has become a day of demand due to information explosion leading to various e-resources to support academics. The users demand to access information at their desktops that too in electronic environment. As a result majority of publishers have started publishing print journals into electronic journals.

The major full text resources available including abstracting databases based on UGC Infonet resources are:

- American Chemical Society (31 Journals)
  http://www.pubs.acs.org/
- Royal Society of Chemistry (23 Journals)
  http://www.rsc.org/
- American Physical Society (8 Journals)
  http://www.aps.org/
- Institute of Physics (36 Journals)
  http://www.iop.org/EJ
- American Institute of Physics (19 Journals)
  http://www.aip.org/
- Cambridge University Press (72 Journals)
  http://journals.cambridge.org/
- Project Muse (222 Journals)
  http://muse.jhu.edu/journals
- J-STOR (293 Journals)
  http://www.jstor.org/
- Kluwer Journals (650 Journals)
  http://www.kluweronline.com/
- Springer Journals (550 Journals)
  http://www.springerlink.com/
- Emerald (28 Journals)
  http://www.emeraldinsight.com
- Nature (1 Journals)
  http://www.nature.com/
- Science Online (1 Journals)
  http://www.scienceonline.org/
- Encyclopaedia Britannica
  http://search.eb.com/
- Elsevier Science (34 Journals)
  http://www.sciencedirect.com/

Abstracting Databases

✦   Chemical Abstracts Service

    http://stnweb.cas.org/

✦   Biological Abstracts

    http://web5.silverplatter.com/webspirsstart.ws? customer=c180470

✦   Royal Society of Chemistry (6 Databases)

    http://www.rsc.org/

✦   Analytical Abstracts

    http://www.rsc.org/is/database/aahome.htm

✦   Catalysts and Catalyzed Reactions

    http://www.rsc.org/is/database/ccrpub.htm

✦   Chemical Hazards in Industry

    http://www.rsc.org/is/database/chihome.htm

✦   Laboratory Hazards Bulletin

    http://www.rsc.org/is/database/lhbhome.htm

✦   Methods in Organic Synthesis

    http://www.rsc.org/is/database/moshome.htm

✦   Natural Product Update

    http://www.rsc.org/is/database/npuhome.htm

e-Portals

✦   Ingenta - Gateway Portal

    http://www.ingenta.com/

✦   J-Gate Gateway Portal - Informatics India Ltd.

    http://www.j-gate.informindia.co.in/

JCCC@CeRA-ICAR www.cera.jccc.in/

Agricultural research, the backbone of agricultural growth in the country, demands timely dissemination of knowledge being generated and updated across the globe from time to time. With the advent of internet facilities and advancement of web technology, almost all reputed international journals are available on-line and can easily be accessed by researchers over the network. Since ICAR is having network connectivity across the institutes and state agricultural universities, select journals could be made available over the network for the use of scientific community. Keeping this broad objective in mind, the NAIP has established the Consortium for e-Resources in Agriculture (CeRA) at the Indian Agricultural Research Institute (IARI). The NAIP is to facilitate accelerated and sustainable transformation of Indian agriculture in support of poverty alleviation and income generation by collaborative development and application of agricultural innovation by the public research organizations in partnership with the farmer's groups, the private sector, the civil society organizations and other stakeholders.

CeRA provides online accessibility of all important journals related to agriculture and biotechnology to researchers and students of the Consortium Partners and timely access to world R and D information and caters to the improvement of the quality of scientific publications, and teaching and research guidance.

CeRA is consortium of e-journals being subscribed by NAIP, ICAR and access is provided to 123 libraries of Agriculture (NARS) for the years 2008-10 (3 years). Through this service the user can access the following three major on-line Portals and Bouquet of Journals from Publishers with full text of an article.

- ☆ Springer link: It is a platform of Springer and product of bouquet of e-journals on different Subjects published by Springer. Through this Bouquet, user can access the full text of around 1100+ journals since 1996.

- ☆ Annual Reviews: Annual Reviews are authoritative, analytic reviews in 34 focused disciplines within the Biomedical, Life, Physical, and Social Sciences *etc.*

- ☆ CSIRO (Australia): Australia's Commonwealth Scientific and Industrial Research Organization (CSIRO)

- ☆ JCCC (J-Gate Custom Content for Consortia): It is a Contents' database collected from journals being subscribed by all 123 Libraries individually for the year 2008 (not through Consortium) under NARS. This database is customized product of M/S Informatics, Bangalore and covers the contents of only periodicals of electronic version and also gives link to approximately 4000+ open access journals since year 2000.

Agris

The Agricultural Resources Information System (AgRIS) is the Central Sector Scheme for Strengthening/Promoting Agricultural Information System in the Department of Agriculture and Cooperation (DAC), Ministry of Agriculture, Government of India. agris.nic.in/agrisportaljuly08.doc

Internet Resources for Agricultural and Veterinary Databases

Veterinary professionals and researchers need information through web sources to accomplish for their research work and patient care. Unfortunately, the Web has a large number of documents that are irrelevant to their work, even those documents that are irrelevant to their work, even those documents that purport to be veterinary related. The Internet and its distributed, unorganized repositories, of information have compounded the problem of information retrieval. In addition to information overload, there is the vocabulary problem with respect to the retrieval of relevant information from systems. Often a veterinary information searcher is uncertain about his exact questions and unfamiliar with veterinary terminology. Veterinary search has several unique requirements that distinguish itself from traditional Web search. The lack – of diversity problem is aggravated by the nature of veterinary web pages. Hence , search results provided by existing medical Web search engines often contain much semantic redundancy, which cannot be easily handled by existing methods for identifying near-duplicate documents of result diversification. To find useful veterinary information, the searcher often has to go through a large number of Web pages laboriously.

Most of the web search engines allow the Searcher to use Boolean logic and truncation in search statements, typically, a search engine works by sending out a spider to fetch as many documents as possible, another program, called an indexer, then reads these documents and creates an index based on the words contained in each document. Each web search engine uses a proprietary algorithm to create its indices such that, ideally, only meaningful results are returned for each query.

Since the conceptualization of ICT, many of its websites are providing information, links and are acting as resource pages for the veterinary sciences. Currently available resources on the web about the veterinary sciences, which are of great research value to the teaching faculty and students in the field of Veterinary Sciences are given below.

Intute (www.intute.ac.uk)

Intute is a gateway to evaluated, quality Internet resources in animal health, aimed at students, researchers, academics and practitioners in animal health.

PubMed (www.ncbi.nlm.nih.gov)

Since July 1997 the National Library of Medicine based in the United States has provided free Internet access to Medline. Many sites now offer Medline access. The Library recommends the official Pubmed site.

Medline (MEDlars onLINE) is a bibliographic database covering the fields of medicine, nursing, dentistry, veterinary medicine, the health care system, and the preclinical sciences. Medline is a massive database of bibliographic citations (*e.g.,* authors, title, and journal reference) and author abstracts from over 3,800 biomedical journals. Medline contains over 9 million records dating back to 1966 and has world-wide coverage, although the majority of citations are in English.

The bibliographic details can be printed off the screen. Ask the Library if you require the full text of the articles.

Animal Science (www.animalscience.com)

This new subscription site replaces the original site. It provides a searchable, comprehensive animal health and production abstract database with 25-year archive and linkage to full text primary journals in the Ingenta Journals system. Subject-focused community areas incorporating discussion forums and the facility for uploading documents. Visitors area with listserves, calendar, bookshop, useful links and much more.

Veterinary Faculty University of Montreal (www.medvet.umontreal.ca)

This database is produced by the University of Montreal and offers access to 125 veterinary journal titles and to 50 conference proceedings. It gives bibliographic details (title, author, journal title *etc.*) and abstracts to veterinary articles.

British Library Integrated Catalogue (http://catalogue.bl.uk)

This catalogue unites a number of previously separate sources to list over twelve million items in the British Library's outstanding collections.

NetVet (http://netvet.wustl.edu/vmla.htm)

NetVet has a comprehensive list of over one hundred e-mail discussion lists to keep abreast of latest developments in their respective field.

Some Useful e-resources on Veterinary Sciences

Examples

☆ http://netvet.wustl.edu/vetmed.htm

☆ http://www.altvetmed.com

☆ http://www.animalscience.com

☆ http://www.bmn.com

☆ http://cahpwww.nbc.upenn.edu

☆ http://cattlepage.com

☆ http://www.msstate.edu.dept/poultry/disbact.html

☆ http://www.msstate.edu/dept/poultry/disviral.html

☆ http://www.msstate.edu/dept/poultry/disproto.html

☆ http://www.ultimateungulate.com

☆ http://vet.cabweb.org

☆ http://www.vet.net

☆ http://www.vet-software.com

☆ http://www.tulance.edu/-dmsander/garryfavweb.html

☆ http://www.ozemail.com.au/-academi

☆ http://www.ianr.unl.edu/pubs/animaldiseases

☆ http://www.aahc.com.au

☆ http://www.avama.org/care4pests/avmaanim.htm

☆ http://www.grandin.com/reference/handle.streess.html

☆ http://avma.org/care4pets

☆ http://www.ghrandin.com/reference/new.corral.html

☆ http://helios.bto.ed.c.uk/mbx/fgn/pnb/filbio.html

☆ http://hammock.ifas.ufl.edu/txt/fairs/49696

☆ http://www.airtime.co.uk/bse/welcome.htm

☆ http://inet.uni-c.dk/-iaotb/bse.htm

☆ http://www.vetmed.auburn.edu/-brockkv/bvdv

☆ http://www.admin.ch/bvet/BSE/Index.html

☆ http://res.ogr.ca/CDRN/main.htm

☆ http://acmepet.com./canine/genetic/index.html

☆ http://funnelweb.utcc.utk.edu/-ypd634/webtopic.html:

☆ http://www.criver.com/techdocs/index.html

☆ http://www.aqualink.com/disease/sdisease.html

☆ http://freespace.virgin.net/larry.taylor/cavtpuk.htm

☆ http://www.ansci.cornell.edu/plants.html

☆ http://www-cyanosite.bio.purduce.edu

☆ http://mendel.berkelley.edu/dog.html

☆ http://www.grandin.com

☆ http://www.ecoli.cas.psu.edu

☆ http://www.avama.org/ezoo

☆ http://members.com/henryhbk/index.html

☆ http://www.Ishtm.ac.uk/mp/bcu/enta

☆ http://www.uky.edu/Agriculture/VetScience/Parasitology/home.htm

☆ http://www.cyberhorse.net.au/csl/tetanus.htm

☆ http://hammock.ifas.ufl.edu/txt/fairs/fairs/49680

☆ http://www.horseshoes.com

☆ http://ss.niah.affrc.go.jp/OIE/FMD/FMD.html

☆ http://www.lib.uiowa.edu/hardin/md/micro.html

☆ http://www.CyberArk.com/animal/holistic.html

☆ http://www.vetmed.ucdavis.edu/gdc/html

☆ http://www.ruu.nl/tropical.ticks

☆ http://agweb.clemson.edu/AgNews/Publications/ADVS/LL17.pdf

☆ www.vetmed.wisc.edu/pbs/johnes

☆ www.uel.ac.uk/pers/d.p.humber/hleish2.html

☆ www.vet.bg.yu/lepto

☆ http://www-sv.cict.fr/bacterio

☆ www.lymenet.org

☆ www.wam.umd.edu/-marky/mastitis.html

☆ www.segi.be/cemu/genetique

☆ www.naturalholistic.com:

☆ http://oncolink.upenn.edu/specialty/vet onc

☆ http://www.biosci.ohio-state.edu/-parasite/home.html

☆ www.life.sci.qut.edu.au/LIFESCI/darben/paraqut.html

☆ www.iah.bbsrc.ac.uk/virus/picornaviridae

☆ http://www.ianr.unl.edu/pubs/animaldisease/nf28.html

☆ www.rabbit.org/faq

☆ http://rotavirus.com

☆ http://numbat.murdoch.edu.au/spermatology/spermhp.html

☆ www.shoal.net.au/-rwylie/tikfaq.html

☆ http://www.parasitology.org

☆ http://cheval.vet.gla.ac.uk/vetscape

☆ http://vin.com/oncology/index.html

☆ http://life.anu.edu.au/viruses/welcome.html

☆ http://www.cvm.edu/wmc

☆ http://biodiversity.bio.uno.edu/-fungi

☆ http://medicine.bu.edu/dshapiro/zool.html

☆ http//www.vet.cornell.edu/consultont/consult.asp

☆ http//www.internets.com/sveterin.html

☆ http//www.nnlm.nih.gov/pnr/samplers/vetmed.html

Homepages of Organizations and Institutions

☆ http//www.cabi.org

☆ http//www.cgiar.org/ilri

☆ http//www.fao.org

☆ http://www.icar.org

☆ http://www.oie.int

☆ http//www.wehn.com

☆ http://www.nic.in/icar/cicfri.html

☆ http://cirg.up.nic.in

☆ http://www.nic.in/ciba

☆ http://gau.guj.nic.in

Bibliographic Databases

It has already been mentioned earlier that many developing countries have their documentation centers which have created their own databases in different fields of agriculture. The advanced countries have brought their agricultural data in electronic, form, where as in India the agricultural information system is still in the formative stage. The Indian agricultural databases on tobacco (CTRI, Rajamundry), Diary (NDRI, Karnal) jute and sun hemp (JTRI, Kolkata), Plantation crops (CPCRI, Karsargod), Agricultural crops (IARI, New Delhi), dryland agricultural (CRIDA, Hyderabad), Potato (CPRI, Simla) *etc.*, are still used in hard copy form. Happily CPRI

(Simla) have created a machine readable database on potato in India comprising over 6000 references from 1901 to date. Here it will be appropriate to make a brief mention of the 'Bibliography of Indian Agriculture' (BIA) created by the Indian Agricultural Research institute Library, New Delhi, which is still handled and used manually.

Bibliography of Indian Agriculture (BIA)

BIA is also termed as Indian Agricultural Reference Media. It is a bibliographic database with author title references with citations on catalogue card form. BIA is being created since 1944 and today it contains about 1, 80,000 references. It covers Indian literature on plant sciences particularly on cereal crops, oilseeds, cotton, fruit and vegetables and medicinal plants.

Bibliographic Database with Title Reference

Before the invention of CD-ROM technology, bibliographic, databases containing bibliographic references, citations etc were issued in printed form. However, most of them are still being published in print form parallel to CD-ROMs Almost of all these databases are computerized and are accessible electronically.

To name a few are following.

☆ Bibliography of Agriculture (USDA, National Agricultural Library, Bethesda, Washington DC). It contains references only but no abstracts.

☆ Agrindex (FAO, Agris, Rome) (1975-1985). It contained references without abstracts.

☆ Science Citation Index (SCI) Institute for Scientific information, Philadelphia, (USA). Science Citation Index is published in 6 series in annual comulations.

☆ Citation Index

☆ Contain only citations (references cited in journals).

☆ Index to Scientific Reviews.

☆ Source Index

☆ Permuterm subject Index

☆ Index of Scientific and Technical Proceedings

Some of the Important Bibliographic Databases

1. CABI Databases: CAB International London has built a computerized bibliographic database with abstracts to the tune of 3 million records since 1973. 1.6 lakhs records are added to in annually by scanning over 11,000 core agricultural journals along with books, monographs, conference proceedings, reports, bulletins, *etc.* It is the largest professionally developed database covering world wide issues in agriculture, forestry, dairy, animal and veterinary science, food and nutrition, *etc.* CABI database is published in 47 printed abstracting journals as well as on CD-ROMs. It is also accessible on Internet. (For details see CABI Abstracting Journals in chapter 10).

2. Agris Database: Agris (FAO, Rome) has built a bibliographic database since 1975. Up to 1985 it was purely a bibliographic reference database, but from 1986 it started indexing abstracts also. Presently, it covers only 21% abstracts indexing. Agris provides worldwide bibliographic coverage of agriculture, forestry, fishery, animal and veterinary science, food and nutrition, environment, *etc.* The Agris database is fully computerized and is accessible on Internet. It is also published on CD-ROMs as well as in print form under title "Agrindex" (monthly service)

3. AGRIKGOLA: Agriculture On-line Access (AGRICOLA) is a bibliographic database created by the National Agricultural Library (USA) since 1970. Today, it is the most comprehensive source of bibliographic citations covering wide range of agricultural and allied subjects – Plant sciences, agriculture, animal sciences, aquaculture, veterinary science, forestry, nutrition, *etc.* It contains 3.3 million citations with abstracts to journal articles, monographs, theses, patents, reports, A-V materials, *etc.* 1,00,000 records are added annually. AGRICOLA is available online at NAL and accessible via the Internet as well on CD-ROMs and magnetic tapes since 1970. Its print version is 'Bibliography of Agriculture'.

4. Biosis Database: Biosis (Bioscience Information Service, Philadelphia) is the world's most comprehensive bibliographic database in the field of bio sciences, including life sciences, genetics, toxicology and zoological literature. Its Biosis Previews database on hard disk contains over 7 million bibliographic records with abstracts since 1985 and is available online as well as on CD-ROMs.

5. Biotechnology Database: Derwent Publications Ltd. Since 1982 have created a computerized database in the field of biotechnology scanning over 1200 world's leading scientific and technological journals. The online database is known as 'Biotechnology Abstracts' and its print version is also issued under title 'Biotechnology Abstracts'. It contains 140,000 Abstracts in the fields of biology biotechnology, chemicals, food and agriculture, genetics, health sciences, pharmaceuticals, plant genetics and breeding and wastes, *etc.*

6. Chemical Abstracts Service (CAS): It is the largest database in the world on chemical science and technology developed by the American Chemical Society (Ohio, USA). Since its beginning in 1907 Chemical Abstracts (CA) has published over 15 million abstracts for the CAS database (15 millionths abstract published on March 7, 1994). CAS online database offers through STN Express a specially designed software package, a number of specific services like:

7. Food and Human Nutrition Database: FAO of the United Nations since 1975 have created bibliographic database which covers, food and agriculture, health sciences and nutrition, *etc.* It contains 3,11,000 records and adds 25,000 abstracts annually.

8. Food Science and Technology Database (FSTA): International Food information Service (IFIS) since 1969 has a world leading Food Science

and Technology database which covers various aspects of food science, food products and food processing including biotechnology, economics, manufacturing, legislation and packaging for any commodity. Based on information from 2000 scientific journals in the line, FSTA database contains about 50,000 abstracts. Its hard disc information is accessible on Internet, in addition to CD-ROM and print copy of 'Food science and Technology Abstracts'.

Chapter 14

Information Security for Academic Library

An Overview

The prominence of information in today's society has led the scholars and leaders to claim the era of information which is shaping the concept of information society, a concept where information dominates new modes of social organization. As our information society evolves, organizations increasingly store, use and distribute information. Information used by organizations is now highly valued and has become an important strategic asset. A strong connection exists in society between growing reliance on electronic Information System and associated technology, which has made information sharing, scholarly communication easier and less expensive. Timely availability of relevant and necessary information is the backbone of every quality research and development process. Today, library environments are increasingly reliant on computer technology. Many libraries of all sizes have discontinued use of card catalogs in favor of electronic versions – and many of the electronic versions previously accessible only via terminals within library buildings are now Web-accessible. Online searching of a plethora of databases and other information sources has become ubiquitous for the end user, rather than being restricted to librarians trained in online searching. Access to general purpose microcomputers and software, as well as to the Internet, is offered in nearly all libraries.

Academic Libraries and Information System

Academic libraries have for a century played critically important roles in supporting research, teaching and learning in all subjects and disciplines within their host universities. Technological developments and the availability of online information sources are welcomed by researchers and librarians both. With the advent of the information era, the rise of digitization and digital library has become the ultimate appearance of modern library today. The digital environment has radically changed the way researchers find articles as well as how they access and retrieve it. University libraries realize the storage of huge capacity and magnanimity of information processing and make library users get huge information resources. The digital library is in essence a multimedia information online repository takes distributed massive groups of information databases as resources, takes the network as transmission platform, and over comes the space and time limitation. However it involves risk and troubles in addition to the great advantages such as hackers and computer virus. Today greater importance is attached to intellectual property rights, which can lead to the embarrassment huge losses if part of secret information is lost.

Concept of Information Security

The concept Information Security includes secure information handballing, processing and use in the fully controlled and protected environment. Although the concept is much related to the application of Information Communication Technology in the processing of information based on computer, microelectronics and telecommunication. With development of various standards the concept information security expanded and encompassed many issues relating security other that ICT, such as building security, water security, fire security, *etc.* Hence today information security is to ensure availability of information, integrity and confidentiality of an information system through avoiding every possible threat and risk which would put these things in danger. Three basic security concepts important to information on the internet are confidentiality, integrity, and availability. Concepts relating to the people who use that information are authentication, authorization, and non-repudiation. When information is read or copied by someone not authorized to do so, the result is known as loss of confidentiality.

Information can be corrupted when it is available on an insecure network. When information is modified in unexpected ways, the result is known as loss of integrity. This means that unauthorized changes are made to information, whether by human error or intentional tampering. Integrity is particularly important for critical safety and financial data used for activities such as electronic funds transfers and financial accounting. Information can be erased or become inaccessible, resulting in loss of availability. This means that people who are authorized to get information cannot get what they need. Availability is often the most important attribute in service-oriented businesses that depend on information.

Availability of the network itself is important to anyone whose activities relies on a network connection. When users cannot access the network or specific services provided on the network, they experience a denial of service. To make information available to those who need it and who can be trusted with it, organizations use authentication and authorization. Authentication is proving that a user is the person he or she claims to be. That proof may involve something the user knows (such as a password), something the user has (such as a "smartcard"), or something about the user that proves the person's identity (such as a fingerprint). Authorization is the act of determining whether a particular user (or computer system) has the right to carry out a certain activity.

Authentication and Authorization

Users must be authenticated before carrying out the activity they are authorized to perform. Security is strong when the means of authentication cannot later be refuted—the user cannot later deny that he or she performed the activity. This is known as *non-repudiation.* The internet users want to be assured that:

☆ They can trust the information they use

☆ The information they are responsible for will be shared only in the manner that they expect

☆ The information will be available when they need it

☆ The systems they use will process information in a timely and trustworthy manner

The technologies of information assurance address system intrusions and compromises to information. In order to ensure foolproof information security system for any information system, the systematic risk assessment requires regularly.

International Standard for Information Security

ISO/IEC 27001:2005 ISO 27001 is an International Standard for information security was published and came into effect on October 15, 2005, that requires organizations to implement security controls to accomplish certain objectives. The standard should be used as a model to build an Information Security Management System (ISMS). An ISMS is part of an organization's system that manages networks and systems. It aims to "establish, implement, operate, monitor, review, maintain, and improve information security" commensurate with the perceived security risks to the business of the organization. As a model for information security, ISO 27001 is a generic standard designed for all sizes and types of organizations including governmental, non-governmental, and non-profit organizations. It requires the managing body of an organization to plan, implement, maintain, and improve the ISMS. The ISMS model ensures the selection of adequate security controls based on organizational objectives to protect all information assets.

The international standard ISO/IEC 27001:2005 has its roots in the technical content derived from BSI standard BS7799 Part 2:2002. It specifies the requirements for establishing, implementing, operating, monitoring, reviewing, maintaining and improving a documented Information Security Management System (ISMS) within an organization. It is designed to ensure the selection of adequate and proportionate security controls to protect information assets. This standard is usually applicable to all types of organizations, including business enterprises, government agencies, and so on. The standard introduces a cyclic model known as the "Plan-Do-Check-Act" (PDCA) model that aims to establish, implement, monitor and improve the effectiveness of an organization's ISMS. The PDCA cycle has these four phases.

(i) "Plan" phase – establishing the ISMS

(ii) "Do" phase – implementing and operating the ISMS

(iii) "Check" phase – Monitoring and Reviewing the ISMS

(iv) "Act" phase – Maintaining and Improving the ISMS

Information Security Practices and Library

Information security, it rather includes issues such as information management, information privacy and data integrity. In a library it would also include personnel security and policies, steps taken for effective backups, and the physical integrity of computing facilities. Information system in university libraries support the delivery of images, scholarly communication, sharing of information, services and collections to local and remote users and this availability over the internet inevitably exposes it to security threats. Information system is an asset for an organization when it is well managed. Security is also very important issue in the designing of digital library. Integrity, confidentiality and availability can be suffered as well hamper. The failures and weaknesses in the system can cost economical loss and can even lead to pain and suffering or other serious problems. Hence appropriate and effective information security control measures ensure the availability, confidentiality and integrity of information system.

Major Categories of the Threats for the Information Security

1. Hacking (Intrusion)

Intrusion is nothing but gaining access to a computer system without the knowledge of its owner. The people who do this kind of unlawful things are called as hackers. Once they get access to targeted systems, they can alter data available on those systems or steal private information such as SSN, personal information and sometimes some sensitive information related to bank and credit card accounts. Most of the targeted systems for hackers are e-Commerce websites, individual machines and sometimes bank websites that provide facility for online banking.

The targeted systems for hacking are depending on the hackers and their personal types. Some people will do hacking just for fun and curiosity. In order to do hacking, hackers has to crawl on the targeted systems and gather the information about its strength, weakness, operating systems used, unsecured folders, shared folders, configuration files *etc.* They will collect all these data and do analysis about how to compromise the targeted website or system. Once they find a way, they will enter through that, and try to exploit the systems. Some hackers use Trojan horse programs to gain access to the targeted systems. Trojan horse programs are very dangerous threats for e-Commerce websites and even for personal machines.

In order to prevent the systems from these kinds of attacks, most of the e-Commerce websites and even single users have started to use good firewall systems; whenever there is an attack, the firewall systems reports immediately and sometimes it helps to track the attack. Hackers can always penetrate firewall systems by some sort of new ways and hence it is always better to conduct a vulnerability test before releasing systems for operation.

2. Viruses and Worms Computer Programs

There is a subtle difference between Virus and Worm; both can replicate itself, but when traveling on the network, Virus needs a carrier file. It can't travel on its own on the network; whereas Worms can travel on its own without anything. It doesn't actually need any infected file to stick in. Viruses and Worms are really annoying problems for all systems. The ultimate aim of these Viruses and Worms is making a good working system to malfunction and sometimes worms can sniff in and steal private information to send it to its creator. As per Trendmicro, so far 60,000 viruses have been identified and 400 new viruses are getting created every month. Earlier days, Viruses were spreading through floppy diskettes. Nowadays, it spreads through Internet, which is a broad gateway for these malicious programs. It can spread quickly and affect all systems in an organization within a minute and can create millions of dollar loss for the organization in a minute.

If the files or mails are not from trusted source, it is better to delete it right away without opening it. The better way to avoid viruses is installing anti-virus software on all systems. Some new viruses may even try to bypass antivirus software; so, it is very important to keep virus-signature-database up to date. In addition to anti-virus software, users should be very careful while downloading files from internet or mails, because that may contain some malicious virus.

3. Trojan Horse Programs

It is initially used for system administration purposes. System administrators used these programs to control their work-stations remotely. These programs are having two components; one runs as a server and another one runs as a client. The server part is installed on the work stations and the client is installed on the administrators? machines. Though it has a good purpose, its power can be used for bad purposes too. Hackers can use these programs to get control on their target machines and watch all the activities. This is very dangerous than Virus and DOS for the e-Commerce businesses.

Threatening Issues with Trozan Horses

☆ It allows for data integrity attack.

☆ It can store key strokes and make it viewable for hackers. As a result, hackers can easily get the victim's login-ids and passwords. This way, it affects confidentiality.

☆ It allows gaining control over the target machine and to steal private information available on the target system. This way it affects privacy policy.

☆ It can be installed very easily on the target machines simply by sending it as an email attachment. Basically, Trojan horse programs affect the very basic principles of information security.

☆ Hackers can see screen shots of targeted machines using Trojan horses. Sometimes, if websites are not secured properly, some third party companies can collect consumer information and pass it to some other businesses. It is a serious threat to customer privacy.

4. Spoofing

The exact meaning of spoofing is deceiving others. It is actually fooling other computer users to think that the source of their information is coming from a legitimate user.

Method of Spoofing:

☆ IP Spoofing

☆ DNS Spoofing

☆ ARP (Address Resolution Protocol) Spoofing

IP Spoofing

IP spoofing changes the source-address of an IP packet to show that it is from a legitimate source, but really it might be coming from a hacker. Thus, the hacker attacks the system and at the same time hides his IP address from the eyes of firewalls. The targeted systems for IP Spoofing are UNIX systems and RPC services. Basically, the services that require IP authentication are the main targets for IP Spoofing.

DNS Spoofing

Directing the users to a different website and collecting personal information through web forms illegally. DNS Spoofing is actually very dangerous threat, because DNS is the one that manages domain names and creates equivalent IP addresses.

ARP Spoofing (ARP Poisoning)

ARP is actually maintaining a table of MAC addresses of all computers connected in a network. Any information that comes to ARP is delivered to respective computer based on the mappings available on the ARP's tables. Suppose, if ARP couldn't find MAC address for a message, it broadcasts a message to all systems to get a reply from the exact destination-machine with its MAC address; when it gets the destination-machine's MAC address, it updates it on MAC table. This is the stage where ARP spoofing can happen. ARP Spoofing actually happens when a hacker (hacker's machine) sends a reply to the ARP's broadcasted message saying that the hacker's machine is the legitimate one. Then, ARP gets hacker's MAC address and add it to its table. As a result, hacker will gain a legitimate connection to the network illegally.

5. Sniffing

Initially, this technique was being used for fixing network problems. Because it can watch network packets, it is now being used by hackers for scanning login IDs and passwords over the wires. TCPDUmp and Snoop are better examples for sniffing tools. The main targeted systems for sniffing attacks are UNIX based systems. The better way to avoid sniffing attack is encryption. If sensitive information is encrypted before sending to wires, hackers can't really understand what it is. They need the key to decrypt the information. So, the information sent over network could always be safe with encryption.

6. Denial of Service (DoS)

This DoS attack is not really used for stealing the information. The main aim of this attack is to bring down the targeted network and make it to deny the service for legitimate users. In order to do DoS attacks, people do not need to be an expert. They can do this attack with simple ping command. Normally, when experienced hackers attack a site with DoS, they won't do the attack directly from their machine. They will install a small program called zombies on some computers those are in intermediate level in the networks; whenever they want to attack, they will run those programs remotely and will make the intermediate computers to launch the attacks simultaneously. If the intermediate computers are more than 1000, the targeted servers will definitely go down because of the overload. Finally, the legitimate users may not be able to get proper service from those affected servers. The remedy would be restarting the servers, but by that time, the owner would have lost valuable time, business and money.

7. Removable Media

Nowadays, USB flash drives, which can easily store information by the Gigabytes, are easily accessible and available at a cheap price. People with malicious intent can use it to download and steal information. Malware developers also use it to distribute malware.

8. Social Engineering Techniques

Social Engineering is designed to attack us, technology users who are considered as the weakest link. Such techniques may include a caller pretending to be an authority figure and demanding a password be reset or an email enticing a recipient to click on a link out of curiosity.

9. Mobile Computing Devices (Smart Phones and Laptops)

Smart phones and laptops have added flexibility and mobility to an organization. However, their small size makes them prone to loss or theft which, in turn, may result in disclosure of information. These devices can also be used to discreetly break into our networks, particularly the wireless ones. Furthermore, these devices can also be used to secretly take pictures and videos or record conversations.

We have better things to do than update our computers and programs. It's not (only) because people are lazy. It's because every layer of security we add causes more work for them. Much of this advice, many of these things we want them to do just costs too much in terms of a daily burden when so few of them will really be harmed by evil doers. There is generally low motivation and poor understanding of why this could be important.

So even though we have better security than ever before, there are also more ways to defeat it than ever before. To make matters worse, we are now in the era of "steal everything." We all have something a hacker is interested in stealing.

Educational institutions that train librarians have changed their emphasis from the relatively narrow world of OPACs and online searching to include the Internet, LAN and server administration, interface design, and programming. However, issues of security and privacy still tend to focus on issues such as risks from troubled patrons, book theft, and censorship. When information security is addressed, it may be from the point of view of corporate information security management, rather than library environments. In the future, consideration of information security issues will likely be seen in basic courses in information technology. Currently, however, information security is often under-appreciated in libraries. It is recommended that steps be taken in all libraries to assess and minimize information security risks. In contrast, many of the challenges associated with academic e-resources are not well known among the users, librarians or university administrators. The difficulties associated with the selection, licensing, acquisition, copyright, DRM, threats, risk and management are greatly underestimated.

Chapter 15

Protecting Copyright in e-Environment

An Overview

Among all the significant advances made by human mind till today, probably the most important is the invention of the concept of Internet. This innovative concept of Internet brought revolutionary transformation and influences in every aspect of human life including the management of library resources. As the present generation live partly in the physical world and partly in the digital world, reaching out and connecting to each other across fiber-optic lines. Likewise, the digital means of production are widely distributed (Mcdermott, 2012). The digital age has signified easier access to knowledge and information. Almost every conceivable source of information is accessible at the click of a button (Jones, 2004). Currently about 40 per cent of world's population makes use of internet. The number of internet users has increased tenfold from 1999-2013 (internetlivestats, 2014). The internet represents a great opportunity for access to content and assists creators by providing a medium for easier dissemination of their works to public (Jones, 2004). Therefore, today most of the libraries changed themselves on par with the changing environment and adopted digitalization of institutional repositories; open archives *etc.*

Copyright

It protects the labour, skill and judgement of author, artist or some other creator, expender in the creation of original piece of work. It may be given for creators of literacy; dramatic; musical and other artistic work and producers of cinematographs and sound recordings. In fact, it is a bundle of rights, including inter-alia, rights of reproduction, communication to the public adaptation and translation of work. A copyright is a set of exclusive legal rights; authors have rights over their works for limited period of time (Indian Copyright Act, 1957).

According to IFLA copyright is "norms grant legal protection for authors and creators to exploit their works, while providing society access to works and thus, encourage innovation, research and further creativity. Legal flexibilities in copyright, known as limitations and exceptions, provide balance in a copyright system between users and creators of protected works (IFLA, 2014). Different countries have different copyright laws. The differences are mostly on whether or not the government's work fall under copyright, the duration of copyright, and the issue of what is and what is not fair use (Wikipedia). Over the years, for libraries, copyright exception and limitations has become increasingly important to serve its users by providing access to knowledge and preserve the scientific and cultural heritage.

Copyright Infringement (Breaking Law)

A copyright infringment disputes are usually resloved through direct negotiation, a notice and take down process, or itigation is a civil court. Intellectual property rights are infringed when a product, creation or invention protected by IP laws are exploited, copied or otherwise used without having the proper authorisation, permission or allowance from the person who owns those rights or their representatives (IPO, UK, 2014). Copyright infringements types are Direct infringement- wholesale reproduction and distribution of copyrighted works. Contributory infringement- users knowingly encouraging infringing activity and Vicarious infringement- a violation which occurs when operator has the ability to supervise users, but chooses not to supervise and control for financial benefits (Wikipedia).

Indian Copyright Act, 1957

Section 51 of the Act, explains Copyright in a work shall be deemed to be infringed:

(a) when any person, without a licence granted by the owner of the copyright or the Registrar of Copyrights under this Act or in contravention of the conditions of a licence so granted or of any condition imposed by a competent authority under this Act –

☆ does anything, the exclusive right to do which is by this Act conferred upon the owner of the copyright, or

☆ permits for profit any place to be used for the communication of the work to the public where such communication constitutes an infringement of the copyright in the work, unless he was not aware and had no reasonable ground for believing that such communication to the public would be an infringement of copyright; or

(b) when any person-

☆ makes for sale or hire, or sells or lets for hire, or by way of trade displays or offers for sale or hire, or

☆ distributes either for the purpose of trade or to such an extent as to affect prejudicially the owner of the copyright, or

☆ by way of trade exhibits in public, or

☆ imports into India, any infringing copies of the work

Provided that nothing in sub-clause (iv) shall apply to the import of one copy of any work for the private and domestic use of the importer.

Explanation:- For the purposes of this section, the reproduction of a literary, dramatic, musical or artistic work in the form of a cinematograph film shall be deemed to be an "infringing copy".

Information Technology Act, 2000

Cyber Laws and Information Technology Act 2000, the Act of Parliament recieved the assent of the President of the 9th June, 2000. Section 43(b) specifically covers that, if any person without permission of the owner or any other person who is incharge of a computer, computer system or computer network downloads, copies or extracts any data, computer data base or information from such computer, computer system or computer network including information or data held or stored in any removable storage medium. It is the primary law in India dealing with cyber crime and electronic commerce.

Digital Millennium Copyright Act

The DMCA act is legislation enacted by the United States congress in october 1998 by the United State copyright law that implements treatise of WIPO. DMCA was an attempt to address piracy where a growing amount of content is available in digital format. With advent of digital resources and internet, copies of information resources could easily made by anyone with a personal computer, and then distribute widely via the web. The doctrine of first sale forbids the making of copies; however, the use of digital resources inevitably involves making a copy. If a user shares, lends, or gives a book or CD to another user, they no longer have access to that content. With digital sharing, the original party retains a copy of that content and therefore retains access (Buchanan and Campbell, 2005). Half a decade after its existence, there is a renewed challenge to assure that copyright law continues to uphold the right balance between protecting creative works and maintaining the benefits of the free flow of information.

Conventions on Copyright and its Principles

The convention concluded in 1886 was revised at Paris in 1896, at Brussels in 1948, at Stockholm in 1967 and at Paris in 1971, and was amended in 1979. The convention is open to all states. Most countries are members of the Berne convention. The Convention rests on three basic principles and a series of provisions determining the minimum protection to be granted, as well as making special provisions available to developing countries which want to make use of them.

Three Basic Principles

1. The principle of "national treatment" *i.e.* works originating from one of the contracting states must be given the same protection in each of the other contracting states.
2. The protection must not be conditional.
3. The protection is independent of the existence of protection in the country of origin of the work (Berne Convention) (Fabunmi, 2007).

Uruguay Round Agreements, 1994 to implement obligations under the Agreement on Trade-Related Aspects of Intellectual Property Rights (TRIPS) of the World Trade Organization (WTO). TRIPS incorporate by reference many obligations under the Berne Convention for the Protection of Literary and Artistic Works. However, TRIP introduced the protection of two categories of works, mainly from the point of view of digital environment, such as computer programs and databases. In Geneva, 1996, the World Intellectual Property Organisation (WIPO) adopted treaties with an objective to grant protection to owners of the copyrights and neighbouring rights with respect to usage of their properties in the digital environment. As large amount of information is born digital and comes in various formats, UNESCO has adopted a resolution in its 31st session (2001) to preserve and safeguard the valuable information and continuing accessibility of ever growing digital information of the world. The adopted Recommendations in 2003, encourages member state to recognise and enact the right of universal online access to public and government information identify and promote repositories of information and knowledge in the public domain and make available to all. It also recognises the importance of fair balance between the interest of right-holders and those of users when works are exploited in the digital environment. The International Federation of Library Associations and Institutions (IFLA) represent the interests of the world's libraries and their users. IFLA supports balanced copyright law that promotes the advancement of society as a whole by giving strong and effective protection for the interests of rights-holders as well as reasonable access in order to encourage creativity, innovation, research, education and learning. It also supports the effective enforcement of copyright and recognises that libraries have a crucial role to play in controlling as well as facilitating access to the increasing number of local and remote electronic information resources. Librarians and information professionals promote respect for copyright and actively defend copyright works against piracy, unfair use and unauthorised exploitation.

Indian Copyright Act, 1957 (Copyright Society)

Be it enacted by Parliament in the Eighth year of the Republic of India. Collective administration of copyright by Copyright Societies (Indian Copyright Act, 1957) is a concept where management and protection of copyright in works are undertaken by a society of authors and other owners of such works. No authors and other owner of copyright in any work can keep track of all the uses others make of his work. It is in the interests of copyright owners to join a copyright society to ensure better protection to the copyright in their works and for reaping optimum economic benefits.

Major Role of Role of Copyright Societies (Indian Copyright Act, 1957) are Issue or Grant of licence. A copyright society can issue or grant licences in respect of any work in which copyright subsists or in respect of any other right given by the Copyright Act. The business of issuing or granting license in respect of literary, dramatic, musical and artistic works incorporated in a cinematograph films or sound recordings shall be carried out only through a copyright society duly registered under this Act. This is a kind of compulsory collective licensing for managing of performing rights.

Major Reasons to Adopt e-environment Friendly Library

The following are the major reasons to adopt e-environment friendly liberary.

☆ To preserve the age old materials for long use which are important and valuable for future

☆ Better and enhanced access to a defined stock of research material.

☆ Support for democratic considerations by making public records more widely accessible.

☆ To give the institution opportunities for the development of its technical infrastructure and staff skill capacity.

☆ Better search and retrieval facilities for library types of materials.

☆ To facilitate new forms of access and use.

☆ Creation of a single point of access to documentation from different institutions concerning a special subject.

Library Manager and e-environment

The expectations and needs of users are very similar in the paper-based and in the e-environment. It is found that users want the information reliably and easily accessible in e-environment and they expect that the integrity of the information they get from the library will be assured (Graham, 1995). As in the paper-based environment, digital services must be "planned, implemented, and supported" (Hastings and Tennant, 1996), and instead of being the "gatekeepers" to material, library managers now follow new directions which were identified by Ching-chih Chen as follows (Chen, 1994) from library-centered to information-centered, from the library as an institution to the library as an information provider, and the librarians as a skilled information specialist functioning in an all-related information environment, from using new technology for the automation of library functions to utilizing technology for the enhancement of information access and delivery of items not physically contained within the four walls of the library and from library networking for information provision to area networking.

Emerging Issues in e-Environment of Librarian

☆ Emergence and developments in technology has brought new kind of resources in to the libraries such as digital resources. It is known that the basic principles of copyright remain the same for the traditional and digital resources. However, the Copyright law has been reformed to face the challenges of the digital environment.

☆ Copyright in digital environment is much more difficult to control because of the ease of creation, modification and distribution of digital copies over networks.

☆ Library managers help copyright holders to protect digital works against copyright infringements. On the other hand they also represent users of protected materials, and have a crucial role to play in ensuring the access to resources regardless of technical innovations (Szczepariska, 2004). The issues of IPR lead challenges in management of digital services in terms of administering complex copyright infringement. This issue became a major challenge for present day libraries; this is an aspect where library managers and users need to take precaution. Intellectual property is one of the challenges to building an effective e-environmental digital library.

☆ It stated that a key element for digital libraries is appropriate recognition and protection of legal rights such as copyright, publicity, privacy, as well as less legalistic but serious concerns associated with the ethics of sharing.

☆ During the recent years, in addition to IPR laws, the contractual licensing is emerging to shape the digital environment and is being used to limit user rights unlike paper materials, digital information generally is not purchased by consumers or the library; rather it is licensed by the library from information providers. A licence usually takes the form of a written contract or agreement between the library and the owner of the rights to distribute the digital information (IFLA, 2013).

☆ The digital technology has influenced on the territorial and temporal framework for copyright licensing. The proliferation of new licensing practices appears to reflect the development of collaborative creativity and a new, more dynamic position of the user in the network environment.

☆ Each user is benefitted by readily available digital technologies and media hardware and software, a potential consumer, producer, creator and distributor of creative work. While licensing is finely tuned for the analog world, the digital environment has changed the way in which copyright content is marketed, distributed, delivered and consumed, and this has had significant consequences for the upstream and downstream processes of rights clearance (WIPO).

☆ The future challenges of copyright is prescribed by the digital and online environment of the information society with the possibility of works protected by copyright being recorded, stored and made available on demand in digital form all over the world through electronic communications networks such as the internet and with the threat of unlimited perfect quality copies being made of them are not therefore a matter of national laws..

Digital Rights Managements (DRM) in e-Environment

☆ The Digital Rights Management (DRM) is a system for protecting the copyrights of data circulated via the internet or other digital media by enabling secure distribution and/or disabling illegal distribution of the data.

☆ Typically it is a system that protects intellectual property by either encrypting the data so that it can only be accessed by authorised users or making the content with a digital watermark or similar method so that the content cannot be freely distributed.

☆ DRM systems may therefore greatly facilitate the trading of digital works by reconciling the properties inherent to the digital instance of a work with the properties that every original work of authorship has been granted with under copyright law. However, DRM systems are usually employed in the context of particular licensing schemes, where what is being sold is not the digital instance of a work but only the right to use the work under the specific terms and conditions of the license (Filippi, 2009).

☆ The extent that DRM system is likely to feature a number of restrictions which extend beyond the scope of the copyright regime, the properties of the work and of the digital manifestation (Elkin-Koren, 2001).

☆ To preserve and make available the cultural and scientific heritage for future generations, the libraries and archives play a crucial role and some of the libraries have legal mandate. DRM jeopardises this role as they have the potential to lock away covered material forever.

☆ The issue of long term preservation carries a real urgency as media must be adapted regularly to new data formats, operating systems and data carriers. In addition, data (*e.g.* music, software, electronic journals) stored in proprietary DRM formats is at much greater risk of being lost once the playback media is no longer available.

☆ Under DRM, there is a great risk that the public record of the future may be distorted. The DRM technologies attempt to control use of digital media by preventing access, copying or conversion to other formats.

Role of Library Managers Professionals

☆ Libraries play an important role in institutions which spans many spheres of copyrights. These libraries house innumerable copyrighted and non copyrighted print and digital resources with the objective to make these materials available to the user community.

☆ Library managers are in a unique middle ground position between the roles of supplier and the consumer. They serve an intermediary role between users and content providers. In doing so, they acquire materials for uses to use and also librarians provide a wide range of information support services. This puts them in the position to be able to access to the entire collection of materials. While providing access to vast majority of copyrighted works that lose market vitality long before the expiration of the copyrights, libraries are also probably the only entities that preserve public domain materials.

☆ The multiple roles of libraries as social organizations address the balance in the law and are shaped by it. The institutional roles of libraries, library managers and their associations necessitate paying close attention to that balance and promote user rights as well as the rights of the creators.

☆ In view of considering that the library managers are at the forefront of providing copyrighted work to the user community, it is imperative that they are aware of the various laws governing the copyright protected works, their limitations and benefits.

☆ They have the absolute authority to prevent the reproduction of the copyrighted works and protect the piracy of the digital works. While ensuring that the rights and privileges of users and creators of copyrighted works are safeguarded, the library manager always is often in the position to advise its user who is unaware that the text to be copied is protected by copyright material.

Glossary

Abstract: "A summary or brief description of the content of another longer work. An abstract is often provided along with the citation to a work."

Almanac: "1. A collection, usually annual, of statistics and facts, both current and retrospective. May be broad in geographical and subject coverage, or limited to a particular country or state or to a special subject. 2. An annual containing miscellaneous matter, such as a calendar, a list of astronomical events, planting tables, astrological predictions, and anecdotes" (Definition from Yale University Library)

Annotation: "1. A note that describes, explains, or evaluates; especially such a note added to an entry in a bibliography, reading list, or catalog. 2. Process of making such notes. Annotation is the end product of making such notes." (Definition from Colorodo State University Libraries)

Archives: "1. A space which houses historical or public records. 2. The historical or public records themselves, which are generally non-circulating materials such as collections of personal papers, rare books, ephemera, *etc.*"

Article: "A brief work – generally between 1 and 35 pages in length – on a topic. Often published as part of a journal, magazine, or newspaper."

Atlas: "A book or bound collection of maps, illustrations, *etc.*; Volume of maps, plates, engravings, tables, *etc.*, which may be used to accompany a text; or it may be an independent publication." (Definition from Colorodo State University Libraries)

Attachment: "A separate file (*e.g.*, text, spreadsheet, graphic, audio, video) sent with an email message."

Authentication: "A security process that typically employs usernames and passwords to validate the identity of users before allowing them access to certain information."

Author: "The person(s) or organization(s) that wrote or compiled a document. Looking for information under its author's name is one option in searching."

Bibliography: "A list containing citations to the resources used in writing a research paper or other document." See also: Reference.

Book: "A relatively lengthy work, often on a single topic. May be print or electronic."

Book stacks: "Shelves in the library where materials—typically books—are stored. Books in the book stacks are normally arranged by call number. May be referred to simply as the "stacks.""

Boolean operator: "A word—such as AND, OR, or NOT—that commands a computer to combine search terms. Helps to narrow (AND, NOT) or broaden (OR) searches."

Browser: "A software program that enables users to access Internet resources. Microsoft Internet Explorer, Netscape Navigator, and Mozilla Firefox are all browsers."

Call Number: "A group of letters and/or numbers that identifies a specific item in a library and provides a way for organizing library holdings. Two major types of call numbers are Dewey Decimal Call Numbers and Library of Congress Call Numbers."

Catalog: "A database (either online or on paper cards) listing and describing the books, journals, government documents, audiovisual and other materials held by a library. Various search terms allow you to look for items in the catalog."

CD: "An abbreviation for compact disc; it is used for storing digital information."

Chat: "The ability to communicate with others, computer to computer, via typed messages."

Check out: "To borrow/rent/loan an item from a library for a fixed period of time in order to read, listen to, or view it. Check-out periods vary by library. Items are checked out at the circulation desk."

Circulation desk: "The place in the library where you check out, renew, and return library materials. You may also place a hold, report an item missing from the shelves, or pay late fees or fines there."

Citation: "A reference to a book, magazine or journal article, or other work containing all the information necessary to identify and locate that work. A citation to a book thus includes its author's name, title, publisher and place of publication, and date of publication." Controlled vocabulary: "Standardized terms used in searching a specific database."

Course reserve: "A selection of books, articles, videotapes, or other materials that instructors want students to read or view for a particular course. Print reserve materials are usually kept in one area of the library and circulate for only a short period of time." See also: Electronic reserve.

Database: "A collection of information stored in an electronic format that can be searched by a computer."

Descriptor: "A word that describes the subject of an article or book; used in many computer databases."

Dial-up: "A device using telephone lines that allows a computer to access the Internet or two computers to communicate."

Dissertation: "An extended written treatment of a subject (like a book) submitted by a graduate student as a requirement for a doctorate."

Document delivery: - A service that retrieves or photocopies information sources for library users." Also see ILLiad, our LibGuide on USC's document delivery system.

Download: "1. To transfer information from a computer to a program or storage device to be viewed at a later date. 2. To transfer information from one computer to another computer using a modem."

E-book (or Electronic book): "To transfer information from a computer to a program or storage device to be viewed at a later date."

Editor: "A person or group responsible for compiling the writings of others into a single information source. Looking for information under its editor's name is one option in searching."

Electronic reserve (or E-reserve): "An electronic version of a course reserve that is read on a computer display screen." See also: Course reserve.

Encyclopedia: "A work containing information on all branches of knowledge or treating comprehensively a particular branch of knowledge (such as history or chemistry). Often has entries or articles arranged alphabetically."

Full-text: "A complete electronic copy of a resource, usually an article, viewed on a computer display screen. The term "full-text" is often used to refer to the electronic version of an article or book that is also published in print."

Hardware: "The physical and electronic components of a computer system, such as the monitor, keyboard and mouse. Hardware works in conjunction with software."

Hold: "A request by a user to a library that a book checked out to another person be saved for that user when it is returned. "Holds" can generally be placed on any regularly circulating library materials through an in-person or online circulation desk."

Holdings: "The materials owned by a library."

HTML (Hypertext Markup Language): "The computer language used to create documents on the World Wide Web so that they are readable by Web browsers."

Hyperlink: "An image or a portion of text which a Web user can click to jump to another document or page on the Web. Textual hyperlinks are often underlined and appear as a different color than the majority of the text on a Web page."

Icon: "A small symbol on a computer screen that represents a computer operation or data file."

Index: "1. A list of names or topics—usually found at the end of a publication—that directs you to the pages where those names or topics are discussed within the publication. 2. A printed or electronic publication that provides references to periodical articles or books by their subject, author, or other search terms."

Instant Messaging (IM): "An Internet-based service allowing real-time, text communication between two or more users. Instant messaging is also known as chat, especially when more than two people are communicating."

Interlibrary Loan (ILL): "A service that allows you to borrow materials from other libraries through your own library." See also: Document delivery.

Internet: "A worldwide network of computer networks that allows for the transmission and exchange of files. The World Wide Web is part of the Internet."

Journal: "A publication, issued on a regular basis, which contains scholarly research published as articles, papers, research reports, or technical reports.: See also: Periodical.

Journal title: "The name of a journal. Journal title is one common search term."

Keyword: "A significant or memorable word or term in the title, abstract, or text of an information resource that indicates its subject and is often used as a search term."

Limits/limiters: "Options used in searching that restrict your results to only information resources meeting certain other, non-subject-related, criteria. Limiting options vary by database, but common options include limiting results to materials available full-text in the database, to scholarly publications, to materials written in a particular language, to materials available in a particular location, or to materials published at a specific time."

Link: See Hyperlink.

Magazine: "A publication, issued on a regular basis, containing popular articles, written and illustrated in a less technical manner than the articles found in a journal."

Microform: "A reduced sized photographic reproduction of printed information on reel to reel film (microfilm) or film cards (microfiche) or opaque pages that can be read with a microform reader/printer."

Mouse: "A device that allows the user to move and click the cursor on a computer screen for different functions."

Multimedia: "Any information resource that presents information using more than one media (print, picture, audio, or video)."

Newspaper: "A publication containing information about varied topics that are pertinent to general information, a geographic area, or a specific subject matter (*i.e.* business, culture, education). Often published daily."

Online Public Access Catalog (OPAC): "A computerized database that can be searched in various ways—such as by keyword, author, title, subject, or call number—to find out what resources a library owns. OPAC's will supply listings of the title, call number, author, location, and description of any items matching one's search. Also referred to as "library catalog" or "online catalog." You can search USC's OPAC (or USC Library's Catalog) here.

Page/Paging: "To summon or call by name" (Definition from The Free Dictionary). If a book or other library item is located at another location, you can page, or "summon" the book to be sent to your location. For example, to obtain a book from Grand Avenue Library, an off-site USC Library, will require you to page the item and pick it up from Leavey Library. This generally takes one business day. For more information on paging from Grand, click here.

PDF: "A file format developed by Adobe Acrobat® that allows files to be transmitted from one computer to another while retaining their original appearance both on-screen and when printed. An acronym for Portable Document Format."

Peer reviewed journal: "Peer review is a process by which editors have experts in a field review books or articles submitted for publication by the experts' peers. Peer review helps to ensure the quality of an information source by publishing only works of proven validity, methodology, and quality. Peer-reviewed journals are also called refereed or scholarly journals."

Periodical: "An information source published in multiple parts at regular intervals (daily, weekly, monthly, biannually). Journals, magazines, and newspapers are all periodicals." See also: Serial.

Primary source: "An original record of events, such as a diary, a newspaper article, a public record, or scientific documentation."

Print: "The written symbols of a language as portrayed on paper. Information sources may be either print or electronic."

Print Card: "A card that enables its user to print from a computer, or to make copies of a document at a photocopy machine. Student ID cards sometimes serve as copy cards." For more information see the "Library Printing and Copying" page.

Proxy server: "An Internet server that acts as a "go-between" for a computer on a local network (secure system) and the open Web. Often checks to determine "right of access" to the secure environment and speeds up requests by caching frequently accessed Web pages. Can also act as a firewall."

Recall: "A request for the return of library material before the due date."

Refereed journal: See Peer reviewed journal.

Reference: "1. A service that helps people find needed information. 2. Sometimes "reference" refers to reference collections, such as encyclopedias, indexes, handbooks, directories, *etc.* 3. A citation to a work is also known as a reference."

Remote access: "The ability to log onto (or access) networked computer resources from a distant location. Remote access makes available library databases to students researching from home, office, or other locations outside the library."

Renew/Renewal: "A lengthening (or extension) of the loan period for library materials."

Reserve: "1. A service providing special, often short-term, access to course-related materials (book or article readings, lecture notes, sample tests) or to other materials (CD-ROMs, audio-visual materials, current newspapers or magazines). 2. Also the physical location—often a service desk or room—within a library where materials on reserve are kept. Materials can also be made available electronically." See also: Course reserve, Electronic reserve.

Scholarly: See Peer reviewed.

Search statement/Search Query: "Words entered into the search box of a database or search engine when looking for information. Words relating to an information source's author, editor, title, subject heading or keyword serve as search terms. Search terms can be combined by using Boolean operators and can also be used with limits/limiters."

Secondary sources: "Materials such as books and journal articles that analyze primary sources. Secondary sources usually provide evaluation or interpretation of data or evidence found in original research or documents such as historical manuscripts or memoirs."

Serial: "Publications such as journals, magazines and newspapers that are generally published multiple times per year, month, or week. Serials usually have number volumes and issues. The words journal, magazine, periodical, and serial may be used interchangeably."

Software: "The programs installed on and used by the components of a computer system (or, hardware)."

Stacks: See Book stacks.

Style manual: "An information source providing guidelines for people who are writing research papers. A style manual outlines specific formats for arranging research papers and citing the sources that are used in writing the paper." See Citation. Also see our Citation Guide LibGuide .

Subject heading: "Descriptions of an information source's content assigned to make finding information easier." See also: Controlled vocabulary, Descriptors.

Thesaurus: "A list of terms which serves as a standardized or controlled vocabulary for identifying, locating, and retrieving information." (Definition from New York Public Library)

Thumb drive: "A small portable device for storing computerized information. A thumb drive can plug into the USB (Universal Serial Bus) port of any computer and store electronic information."

Title: "The name of a book, article, or other information source."

Upload: "To transfer information from a computer system or a personal computer to another computer system or a larger computer system."

Uniform Resource Locator (URL): "The unique address for a Web page which is used in citing it. A URL consists of the access protocol (http), the domain name (www.nmsu.edu), and often the path to a file or resource residing on that server."

User ID: "A number or name unique to a particular user of computerized resources. A user ID must often be entered in order to access library resources remotely."

Virtual reference: "A service allowing library users to ask questions through email or live-chat as opposed to coming to the reference desk at the library and asking a question in person. Also referred to as "online reference" or "e-reference.""

Wireless: "The name given to any electronic device that sends messages through space via electric or electromagnetic waves instead of via power cords."

World Wide Web: "A network of information, as a part of the Internet, that includes text, graphics, sounds, and moving images. Also know as the Web or WWW or W3. It incorporates a variety of Internet tools into one method of access, such as the Web browser Internet Explorer, Safari, or Firefox."

Zip drive/zip disk: "Devices used in the creation of compressed (or "zipped") electronic information."

References

Annual Report. (2007). Ahmedabad: INFLIBNET, p.iii.

Armstrong, C. J., Edwards, L. and Lonsdale, R. (2002). Virtually there? E-books in UK academic libraries. Program: electronic library and information systems 36 (4): 216-227.Lee, S. D. (2002). Building ans.

Bar-Ilan, J. (2004). The use of Web search engines in information science research. ARIST, 38, 231-288.

Bing Liu (2007). Web Data Mining: Exploring Hyperlinks, Contents and Usage Data: Springer.

Bishop, M. (2003). Computer Security Art and Science: Boston: Pearson Education, Inc.

Boxen, J. (2008). Library 2.0: A Review of the Literature. Reference Librarian, 49(1), 21-34. Retrieved from Library, Information Science and Technology Abstracts with Full Text database.

Breeding, M. (2003). Protecting your library's data. Computers in Libraries. Available at http://www.librarytechnology.org/diglibfulldisplay.pl?SID=201101166 54235839 and ode=bib and RC=10343 and Row=31 and. McClure, S., and Shah, Saumil and Shah, Shreeraj (2003). Web Hacking : Attacks and Defense. Boston: Pearson Education, Inc.

Buchanan, E. and Campbell, J. (2005). New threats to intellectual freedom: the loss of the information commons through law and technology in US. in R.A. Spinello and H.T. Tavani (Eds.), Intellectual property rights in a networked world: theory and practice, Information Science Publishing, pp 225-242.

Cataldo, Tara. T and Buhler, Amy G. (2012). Positively Perplexing E-books:Digital Natives' Perceptions of Electronic Information Resources. Proceedings of the Charleston Library Conference. http://dx.doi.org/10.5703/1288284315106

Chen, C. (1994). Information Super Highway and the Digital Global Library: realities and challenges, Microcomputers for Information Management Vol. 11 no. 3, pp. 143-155

Chhotey, Lal. (1998). Agricrultural Libraries and Information Systems. New Delhi:R.K.Teckno Science Agency.157 to 175p.

Chhotey, Lal and Bhatia, S. (1993). Adoption of Information Technology by Agricultural Libraries in India. Annals of Library Science and Documentation, 40(1): 4-11.

Committee on Copyright and other Legal Matters (CLM). The IFLA Position on Copyright in the Digital Environment, August 2000. http://archive.ifla.org/III/clm/p1/pos-dig.htm.

Copyright issues for libraries (IFLA, 2014) http://www.ifla.org/copyright-issues-for-libraries

Copyright policy, creativity and innovation in the digital economy, The Dept of Commerce Internet policy Task Force, USA, 2013.

Correa, C. (2000). Fair Use in the Digital Era. Paper presented at the UNESCO's INFOethics 2000 Congress on the Theme- Right to Universal Access to Information in the 21st century.

Dhingra, Navjyoti and Mahajan, Preeti, 2007. Use of electronic journals: A case study of Panjab University Library. In: Proceedings of International Caliber, Ahmedabad, Inflibnet, p. 744-755

Divakar, P. (2012). From Plato to Michael Hart: The long journey of e-books. DESIDOC Journal of Library and Information Technology, 32 (2), 109-115.

Electronic Resources Collection Development Policy: Texas State Library and Archives Commission. http://www.texshare.edu/programs.academicdb/collectionpolicy.html accessed on 27th Sept., 2009.

Elkin-Koren, N. (2001). Privatization of Information Policy. Ethics and Information Technology, 2.

Elsevier, 2005. How libraries are training users on e-resources: Best practices. Library Connect, 6(1): 8.

Ezela, L.O.(2009). Effectiveness of Library Resources in the Libraries of Agricultural Research Institutes in Nigeria. Library Philosophy and Practice. February 2009.

Fabunmi, B.A. (2007). The Roles of Librarians in Copyright Protection in Nigeria, International Journal of African and African American Studies Vol. 6 No. 1, pp. 84-93

Fagan, Jody Condit, 2009. Marketing the virtual library. Computers in Libraries. 29(1): 49.

Filippi, P.De. (2009). Copyright in the digital environment from intellectual property to virtual reality. Social Science Research Network, pp. 79-106 http://papers.ssrn.com/sol3

Fox, Edward and ElSherbiny (2011). Security and digital libraries. In Huang, Kuo Hung (Ed.), Digital Libraries- Methods and Applications (pp. 151-160), Intech. Retrieved from www.intechopen.com/books/digital-libraries-methods-and-applications/security-and-digital-libraries

Gauntner Witte, G. (2014) Content Generation and Social Network Interaction within Academic Library Facebook Pages. Journal of electronic Librarianship, 26 (2), pp. 89-100.

Gopal, Krishan 2000. Modern Library Automation. Delhi: Authorspress, p. 94.

Golwal, Madan D., Sonwane, Shashank and Vaishnav, A.A., 2007. Use analysis of electronic journals. In: Digital Media and Library Information Services. IASLIC, Kolkata, p. 663-669.

Gowda, Vasappa and Shivalingaiah, D., 2007. Training needs of researchers in the changing information environment: A case study of university libraries in Karnataka. In: Digital Media and Library Information Services. IASLIC, Kolkata, p. 398-403.

Graham, P.S. (1995). The digital research library: tasks and commitments. In: Digital Libraries '95, Austin, Texas, 11-12 June 1995. http://csdl.tamu.edu/DL95/papers/graham/graham.html

Greg Downey and Sarah, R. (2006). Retrieved from http://uncoveringinformationlabor. blogspot.com/2006/04/informatics-information-science-and.html. Retrieved on 23.11.2014.

Guidelines for UGC-INFONET Digital Library Consortium.

Gupta, Jatinder N.D. and Sharma, Sushil K.C. (2009). Handbook of research on information security and assurance. [Adobe Digital Editions]. Retrieved from www.cs.nott.ac.uk/~jpt/papers/harias.

Harter, Stephen p. (1998), "Scholarly Communication and Electronic Journals: An Impact study," JASIS, 49(6)

Hastings, K. and Tennant, R. (1996). How to build a digital librarian, D-Lib Magazine November,1996 http://www.dlib.org/dlib/november96/ucb/11hastings. html.

Holt, G.E. (2007). Theft by library staff. The bottom line: managing library finances, 20 (02),85-92.

Hombal, S.G. and Prasad, K.N. (2012). Digital copyright protection: issues in the digital library environment. DESIDOC Journal of Library and Informtion Technology, 32(3), pp 233-239.

Horony, Mark D. (1999). Information system incidents: The development of damage assessment model (Master's thesis). Air Force Institute of Technology, Air University, USA.

Hornby, A.S. (2000). Oxford advanced learner's dictionary of current English. Oxford: OUP, p.263.

https://en.wikipedia.org/wiki/ICT_in_agriculture accessed on 28.11.2015

http://www.webworld.unesco.org/infoethics2000/documents/paper_correa.rtf

http://www.bbk.ac.uk/linkinglondon/resources/esystemsdownloads/report_
January2011_The_Use_of_Eresources_among_Linking_London_partners_
Continuum.pdf(Access on 5th Dec.2015)

http://www.epao.net/epSubPageExtractor.asp?src=education.Scientific_
Papers.ICT_its_roles_in_Fisheries

https://archive.org/details/UseOfInformationAndCommuniction
TechnologyToolsictsInFisheries and ei=HBb9JzsZ and lc=en-IN and
geid=7 and s=1 and m=502 and ts=1443873162 and sig=APONPFlOGikx1
W2g6jr5GahD2ZSZzb6LBw(Access on 8th Dec.2015)

http://nectar.reportbee.com/why-ict-is-the-prime-need-of-our-education-system/
(Access on 5th Dec.2015)

http://www.bar.gov.ph/digest-home/digest-archives/69-2007-4th-quarter/3150-
oct-dec07-revolutionizing-the-agriculture-and-fisheries-sector-through-ict and
ei=HBb9JzsZ and lc=enIN and geid=7 and s=1 and m=502 and ts=1443873162
and sig=APONPFkijYaVRGbiQybWKFRSWsJuinZBhw(Access on 7th
Dec.2015)

http://topfishingsites.com/access(Access on 16/11/2015)

http://www fao.org/f/asfa/(Access on 3rd Dec.2015)

http://www.icar.org.in (Access on 4th Dec.2015)

http://www.fao.org (Access on 9th Dec.2015)

Indian Copyright Act, 1957 Sections 13-14, 23-29, 33-36(A)

Intellectual property crime and infringement. Intellectual Property Office, UK, 2014.
http://www.gov.uk/intellectual-property-crime-and-infringment Information
Act, 2000 Section 43.

Internetlivestats (2014) http://www.internetlivestats.com/internet-users/

Jacobs, J., and Clemmer, L., and Dalton, M., and Rogers, R., and Posluns, J (2003).
SSCP: Systems Security Certification Practitioner: Rockland: Syngress
Publishing, Inc.

Jain, P. K. and Kaur, Harvinder (2007) LIS education in India: challenges for students
and professionals in the Digital Age. Malaysia: Malaya University. 481-488.

Javed Mostafa (February 2005). "Seeking Better Web Searches". Scientific American
Magazine. http://www.sciam.com/article.cfm?articleID=0006304A-37F4-
11E8-B7F483414 B7F0000.

Jayade, K. G.; Khot, P. G.(2014): Impact of ICT and mobile technology in agriculture in
Maharashtra. International Journal of Emerging Technologies in Computational
and Applied Sciences (IJETCAS), p.428-432. http://iasir.net/IJETCASpapers/
IJETCAS14-453.pdf accessed on 28.11.2015

Jones, C.S.A. (2004). The Rights, Responsibilities and Liabilities of the Information Provider: The Development of Guidelines. http://www.caribank.org/uploads/publications-reports/research/conference-papers/intellectual-propertydebate/INTELLECTUALPROPERTYJones.pdf

Kamani, K.C.; Kathiriya, D.R. and Parsania, P.S. (2014): AGROPEDIA: An ICT Initiative in Agricultural Extension. Guj. J. Ext. Edu. Vol. 25, p.98-103. http://gjoee.org/volume/Volume_25_ 1.pdf#page=110, accessed on 28.11.2015.

Kawatra, P. S. and Sing, N. K. (2006). E-Learning in LIS education in India. IN proceedings of the Asia-Pacific conference on Library and Information education and Practice, 3-6 April 2006, Singapore.

Kebede, Gas haw. "The Changing Information needs of users in electronic information environments". The Electronic Library, 20(1), pp 41-47.

Kesha Ram, Gordhan Singh Bhati and J.K.Patel. (2014): Dynamic Personality of Farmers and Their Attitude Towards Use of Kisan Call Centre. Guj. J. Ext. Edu. Vol. 25, p.104-107. http://gjoee.org/volume/Volume_25_1.pdf#page=110, accessed on 28.11.2015.

Khandwala, Vidyut. New Approach to Objectives of Library Education. ILA Bulletin. V 4; 1968.p.105 16.

Kovatcheva, Pavlinka From Web 2 to Web 3: Yesterday, Today and Tomorrow. Where is the technology taking us? In UJ LIC Conference: The Future is Now 18 May 2010.

Kukreja, A. and Chakranborti, B. Agricultural Knowledge management and Dissemination: Initiatives by Information and Communication Technology. Journal of Global Communication. 6 (1) Jan-June 2013.

Kumar, Krishan. Library Education in India in the 1960's. Library Herald. V 13; 1971. p. 79-89

Kumar, P.S.G.(2003) Foundations of Library and Information Science: Paper I of UGC Model Curriculum. Delhi: B.R. Publishing.

Kumar, P.S.G., 2006. A Student's Manual of Library and Information Science (on the lines of the Net syllabus of UGC). B.R. Publishing Corporation, Delhi.

Kumar, B.D. and Gururaj Hadagali, S., 2007. "Collection development policy in academic libraries in changing environment: Problem and perspectives". Peal, (1), Jan-Mar, pp. 33-43.

Kumar, P. S. G. (2012). Foundations of Library and Information Science (2nd Ed.,). New Delhi:B R Publication.

Labhasetwar, Milind K., 2007. Use of electronic journals by the faculty members of JDIET Yavatmal. In. Digital Media and Library Information Services. IASLIC, Kolkata, pp. 375-377.

Lancaster, F.W. (1995), "The Evolution of Electronic Publishing." Library Trends, 43(4), pp.518-527.

Larsen, G. (2005). Continuing professional development: trends and prospective in a Nordic context. IN 71st IFLA general conference and council, 14-18 August, 2005, Norway.

Leahy, Phil, 2009. Athens Access management system (Available at: http//72.14235.132/search?q=cache;azi96BbBYKUJ:www.athensams. net/~/media/at hens/ppt/britishcouncil_march03 per cent 2520 ppt. ashx+Athens+access+ management+system&hl = en&ct = 5) (Accessed on 22.1.2009).

Lee, Stuart D (2002). Building an electronic resource collection: A practical guide. London: Library Association Publishing.

Levene, Mark (2005). An Introduction to Search Engines and Web Navigation: Pearson.

Lisa M Cespedes (2014): How ICT tools are improving efficiency of agricultural development. http://www.theguardian.com/global-development-professionals-network/2013/jan/24/data-collection-evaluation-technology-agriculture, accessed on 28/11/2015.

Library and Information Statistics Unit (LISU), (2003) Loughborough University Annual Library Statistics.

Limitations and Exceptions to Copyright and Neighbouring Rights in the Digital Environment: An International Library Perspective (IFLA, 2004), Updated in January 2013. http://www.ifla.org/publications/limitations-and-exceptions-to-copyright-and-neighbouring-rights-in-the-digital-environm.

Lowry, C.B. and Goetsch, (2001).Creating a culture of security in the university of Maryland libraries. Portal: Libaraies and Academy, 01 (04), 455-465.

Lombardo, N., Mower, A., and McFarland, M. (2008). Putting Wikis to Work in Libraries. Medical Reference Services Quarterly, 27(2), 129-145. doi:10.1080/02763860802114223.

Lucy A, Tedd (2005). E-books in academic libraries : An international overview. New Review of Academic Librarianship, 11 (1), 57-79. (http://dx.doi. org/10.1080/13614530500417701).

Luijendijk, W., 1969. Archiving Electronic Journals: The serial Information Provider's Perspective (IFLAJ 22) pp. 209-210.

Lynch, Clifford A. (2001). Metadata Harvesting and the Open Archives Initiative. ARL Bimonthly Report 217, August 2001.

Mahalakshmi P *et al.*, Use of information technology in aquaculture research and management, Fishing Chimes, 24 (9) (2004) 50-53.

Mahapatra, R.K. (2012). Digital Contents Creation and Management in Agricultural Libraries: Issues and Trends. DESIDOC Journal of Library and Information Technology. Vol.32, No.1, January 2012.

Mahapatra, G. (2006). LIS education in India: Emerging paradigms, challenges and propositions in the digital era. Presented at the Asia-Pacific Conference on

Library and Information Education and Practice. 2006 (A-LIEP 2006), Singapore, 3-6 April 2006.

Malwad, N.M. et al. eds. (1996). Digital Libraries. New Delhi: New Age International Ltd. Publishers. Pp28-29.

Manjunath, G. K. (2006). Does IT make you mighty? Time to blend librarianship with pertinent IT skills.

Mathan, Inder Vir and Gupta, Urmil. Need for Rethinking on Library and Information Science Education in India. ILA Bulletin. V.(24)1989.p.208.

McDermott, A.J. (2012). Copyright: regulation out of line with our digital reality. Information Technology and Libraries, pp. 7-20

Meadow. C.T. (1988), "Back to Future: Making and Interpreting the Database Industry Timeline."Database, 11(5), pp14-16.

Mogge, D. (1998) "ARL Directory Tracks Growth in E-publishing."ARL Newsletters, 196, pp.1-2.

Moghaddam, Golnessa Galyani and Talawar, V.G., 2008. Use of scholarly electronic journals at the Indian Institute of Science: A case study in India. Interlending and Document Supply, 36(1): 15-29.

Mortensen, E. (2013). Copyright law, digital media and libraries. http://mysite. pratt.edu/~emortens/projects/copyright.paper.pdf.

NBSS and LUP(2015): Vision2050, ICAR-NBSS and LUP, Nagpur, 23p.

Newby, Gregory (2002). Information security for libraries: IRM press. Retrieved from www.petascale.org/papers/library-security.pdf

Norm Medeiros and Linda Millers *et al.*, 2008. White paper on interoperability between acquisition prepared by sub committee of the Digital library Federation. Electronic Resources Management Initiative Phase. II.

Onatola, A. and Dina, T. (2005/2006). Nigerian Libraries and the Protection of Author's Rights, Nigerian Libraries: Journal of the Nigerian Library Association, Vol. 39, pp. 49-64.

Oppenheim, Charles 1999. "What is the hybrid library." Journal of Information Science,: 97-112.

Peacock, J. (2000). Teaching skills for teaching librarians: post cards from the edge of the educational paradigm. IN COMLA seminar2000: user education for user empowerment, 19-20 October, New Zealand.

Potter, W. (1997). Recent trends in state wide academic library consortia. Library Trends, 45(3), pp.417-419.

Publishers, copyright and Open Access (2010). Open Access Scholarly Information Sourcebook (OASIS). http://www.openoasis.org/index.php?option= com_content and view=article and id=550

Raghavan, K.S.(1998). Library and Information Science Education. V 2. Delhi: Ess Ess.

Ralston, Anthony and Reilly, Edvin D. (1993). Encyclopaedia of Computer Science, 3rd London: Chapman and Hall.Pp413-14.

Ramaiah, Chennupati K. (2012). E-books: Past, present and future. DESIDOC Journal of Library and Information Technology, 32 (2), 79-82.

Ramaiah, Chennupati K. (2012). Users' Perception about E-books in India. DESIDOC Journal of Library and Information Technology, 32 (2), 86-94.

Ramesha, and Ramesh Babu B. (2007). Trends, Challenges and Future of Library and Information science Education in India. DESIDOC Bulletin of Information Technology. 27, 17-26.

Ranganathan, S.R., 1931. The Five Laws of Library Science. Madras Library Association, Madras.

Rao, Y. Srinivasa and Choudhury, B.K. (2008). Information Technology services (ITs): role of information practitioners. Information Age, 2(1), pp. 5-11.

Rao, S.S. (2005). Electronic books: Their integration into library and information center. Electronic Library, 23(1), 116-40.

Rao, N.H. (2004). Integrating Information and Communication Technologies into Agricultural Education and Research in India. University News. 42(12), 22-25.

Reitz,M (2005).Dictionary for Library and Information Science. London:Raintree.

Ross, Nancy; Wolfram, Dietmar (2000). "End user searching on the Internet: An analysis of term pair topics submitted to the Excite search engine". Journal of the American Society for Information Science, 51(10): 949–958.

Rathinasabapathy, G. et al. (2008). E-Journal consortia for agricultural/veterinary universities and ICAR institutes in India. In: National Seminar of IASLIC (23rd: 2008). Proceedings. pp. 90-91.

Saravanan, R. and Suchiradipta Bhattacharjee(2013):Mobile Phone and Social Media for Agricultural Extension: Getting Closer to Hype and Hope? International Conference on Extension Educational Strategies for Sustainable Agricultural Development. A Global Perspective: December 5-8, 2013, University of Agricultural Sciences, Bangalore, INDIA. P. 140-147. http://www.saravananraj.net/wp-content/uploads/2014/12/43_ Mobile_ Phone_ and_Social_Media_ for_Agricultural_Extension-Saravanan-Raj.p

Satyanarayana, M. (2005). INFLIBNET: its activities in library automation. IASLIC Bulletin, 50(2), pp.110-115. Potter, Ben (2015): 87 per cent of farmers will own a smartphone by 2016. http://www.agweb.com/article/87-of-farmers-will-own-a-smartphone-by-2016-naa-ben-potter. Accessed on 26.11.2015.

Sathyaprakash, Behera Jeetendra Kumar and Dr. Singh 2011. Problems and Challenges in Collection Developments of Indian Libraries in Digital Era - An Assessment,. 133-143.

Sen Gupta, Benoyendra. Library Education in India: Let us look hard at it. ILA Bulletin.V4,1968;p.72

Services Collection Development: Electronic Resources Collection Development Policy. As per recommendation from Dr. K.M. Kumar as of January, 2008. http://lib.hku.hk/cd/policies/erp,htm accessed on 27th Sept., 2009.

Seth, M.K and Ramesh, D.B. Library Education through Open University System: Challenges for Library Professionals in India. ILA Bulletin. V32, 1997. p.5

Seetharama, S. and Ambuja, R., 2000. "Collection development in an electronic era". DRTC Annual Seminar on Electronic Sources of Information, 1-3 March, pp. 1-10.

Shah, S.A. (2002). Copyright law – national and international scenario. http://advshah.blogpost.in/2012/09/copyright-law-national-and.html.

Sharma, Rakesh Mani (2012). E-books-Issues and concern of different stake holders in India. Indian Journal of Agricultural Library and Information Services, 28(2), 40-48.

Sharma, Neelam (2012). Automation and digitization in university libraries: a comparative study of seven north Indian university libraries. International Journals of Information Dissemination and Technology, 02 (02), 135-145 Retrieved from www.ijidt.co/index.phd/ijidt/article/view/152/81.

Sharma,Jaideep. Professional Competencies, Employer Expectation and Curriculum for LIS Education in India. ILA Bulletin. V.38;2000.p.181

Sharma, J.B(1996) Elements of Library Science. New Delhi: Kanishka.

Sharma, R. K. (2013).Changing Scenario of Library and Information Science Education in India. New Delhi: Ess Ess Publication.

Singh, Jagtar. Globalization of Library and Information Science Education via the Internet. Library Herald. V 39;2001.p.71.

Singh, Surendra.(2000) Trends in Library and Information Science. New Delhi: Gyan Publishing.

Siva Balan, K.C. (2015): Instant advice on fertilizer dose to farmers: Smartphone app from India. http://www.e-agriculture.org/es/node/65717. Accessed on 26.11.2015

Skills through LIS Education. Retrieved from http://eureka.lib.teithe.gr:8080/bitstream/handle/10184/4102/Skills per cent 20through per cent 20LIS per cent 20education.pdf?sequence=1. Retrieved on 20.11.2014.

Steve Lawrence; C. Lee Giles (1999). "Accessibility of information on the web". Nature, 400 (6740): 107.

Szczepanska, B. (2004). Digital is not different- copyright in digital environment. Proceedings of the IATUL Conferences http://www.iatul.org/doclibrary/public/Conf_Proceedings/2004

Taher, Mohamed; and Davis, Donald Gordon Jr. (1994),"Librarianship and library science in India". Concept publishing Company, New Delhi. pp.108.

The Berne Convention for the Protection of Literary and Artistic Works, usually known as the Berne Convention, is an international agreement governing copyright, which was first accepted in Berne, Switzerland, in 1886.

Thornton, Glenda A., 2000. Impact of electronic Resources on collection development, The role of librarians and library Consortia. Library Trends/Spring., 48(4): 482-456.

UGC-INFONET Digital Library Consortium: A compendium for member institutions. (2008). Ahmedabad: INFLIBNET, p.2. df.

UGC (1993). Report of the Curriculum Development Centre in Library and Information Science, New Delhi:UGC,1993.

UNESCO: Guidelines for the preservation of digital heritage, March 2003. http://unesdoc.unesco.org/images/0013/001300/130071e.pdf

US Code- 17 U.S.C. § 108(b), 2000 (Detailing libraries rights to reproduce and distribute copyrighted works).

Vibhuti, N.B. (2003). Need for Networking in Agriculture Libraries and Information Centres. ILA Bulletin. 39 (3), p.33-36.

Vijaykumar, JK and Manju Das (2000) CD-ROM to DVD-ROM: a new era in electronic publishing of Databases and Multimedia Reference Resources. IASLIC Bulletin, 45(2) pp.49-54.

Vijaya Kumari, J. Changing Scenario in Library and Information Science Education in India : Some Observations. Herald of Library Science. V. 40; 1995. p. 169.

Visakhi, P. *et al.,* 2010. Knowledge Management: Issues and Strategies. U-Day Publisher, New Delhi.

Warrier, Nirupama, J Shivarama and Angadi Mallikarjun (2015). Role of Library and Information Professionalsm. Web 3.0 Era In 10 th International CABLIBER j137.

Wikipedia (http://www.wikipedia.org).

World Bank. (1998). Knowledge for Development: World Development Report. The World Bank/Oxford University Press.

World Bank. (2008). Agriculture Development: World Development Report. The World Bank/Oxford University Press.

World Intellectual Property Organization (WIPO). Copyright Licensing in the Digital Environment. http://www.wipo.int/copyright/en/activities/copyright_licensing.html.

Websites

1. http://www.inflibnet.ac.in/econ/(July 11, 2012)
2. http://www.inflibnet.ac.in/econ/members.php (July 11, 2012)
3. http://www.inflibnet.ac.in/econ/(July 10, 2012)
4. (http://www.inflibnet.ac.in/econ/) (July 11, 2012)
5. http://www.inflibnet.ac.in/econ/(July 10, 2012)

Index

D

Data liberation initiative (DLI) 6

DD Kisan 72

Denial of service (DoS) 121

Department of agriculture and cooperation (DAC) 78, 106

Digital contents 85, 144

digital dissemination 87

Digital libraries 141

Digital millennium copyright act 125

Digital preservation 88

Digital resources management 55

Digital rights managements (DRM) 129

Digitization 85, 116, 147

Discussion forums 102

DNS spoofing 120

Document delivery service 103

Document e-book 64

E

e-agriculture 8

e-banking 9

e-books 1, 27, 30, 63-68, 139, 144, 146, 147

Ebsco 5, 7, 29

Ecofriendly learning tool 63, 65

e-collection 11, 51, 53, 55

e-commerce 11, 118, 119

e-Granth 13

e-journal 1

e-learning 15

Electronic books 30, 63, 65

Electronic collection 6

Electronic information delivery 53

Electronic journal evaluation 5

Electronic newspapers 27

Electronic Resource funding 7

Electronic resources 67, 68, 69

e-mail 17, 101

endorsement 2

e-Portals 105

EPUB 65

e-resources 1, 27, 28, 31, 57-65, 68, 104, 108, 122, 140

e-seva 21

e-technology 71-75

F

Facebook 71, 72, 141

FAOSTAT database 84

File transfer protocol (FTP) 101

Fisheries 77

Food and human nutrition database 112

Food science and technology database (FSTA) 112

Full-text databases 68

G

Gateway 4

Gateway internet access service (GIAS) 98

Geographic information systems (GIS) 73

Global agricultural information 84

Global digital library for agriculture 89

Global positioning system 73

H

Hacking 118, 139

Handheld e-book 65

Higher education libraries 67, 69

HTML e-book 64

Human resource management 41

I

ICAR 86, 88, 145

INDEST 59